Holy Spirit
CONVERGENCE

Keep lifting Jesus up
by the power of the
Holy Spirit —

Pete Battjes

Romans 15:13

1

Holy Spirit Convergence
Copyright 2016 by Dr. Pete Battjes

Occasionally, there will be quotes from other translations and each will be noted as such: New International Version (NIV); New King James Version (NKJV); King James Version (KJV); English Standard Version (ESV).

ISBN 978-0-692-61628-4

Printed in the United States of America

Contact Information:

drpetebattjes@gmail.com

To **Vivian Raye**, my faithful wife and partner in ministry. You have encouraged me in each assignment Jesus has given me. I cherish you and the many adventures we've experienced together through the leading of the Holy Spirit.

To **Youth With A Mission** (YWAM) leaders throughout the world who have faithfully followed the call of God and impacted countless lives in fulfilling the Great Commission of Jesus Christ. May you continue to persevere by faith, through the power and leading of the Holy Spirit, for the glory of God.

> *"It is the Spirit who gives life…"*
>
> **Jesus Christ**
> **(John 6:63 NASB)**

Contents

Foreword

Like many of us, I grew up ignorant about the Holy Spirit. The Spirit was either a "ghost" that was mysterious, an "it" that I couldn't relate to, or something or Someone totally irrelevant to my life.

In fact, for a few years I had an unconscious bitterness toward the Holy Spirit because I'd been taught early in my Christian walk that the so-called Holy Spirit manifestations were of the devil and I'd better stay away from them.

Then one day I found myself in New Zealand, seeking to get to know God, and being prayed for by a man named Blythe Harper who led the "Jesus Marches" in the nation during the 1970's. He prayed that the Holy Spirit would come upon me, deliver me from my bitterness, draw me closer to Jesus, and release His gifts in me.

Bondage was broken. God's power came upon me with a physical manifestation. And all of those things came wonderfully true – beginning that very day.

Now I'm a firm believer in the Person of the Holy Spirit.

Notice the carefully chosen and capitalized word "Person". When we believe the false concept that the Holy Spirit is an it or thing, then we miss His thoughts, feelings, and actions coursing through our being. Only personalities have minds, wills, and emotions that we can have a relationship with.

And "Person" is capitalized in honor of the Holy Spirit being a member of the Triune God – revealed in the New

Testament as Father, Son, and Holy Spirit. The Trinity *created* the world, *redeemed* it through the death and resurrection of the Son, and is now *transforming* it person by person through the indwelling power of the Holy Spirit.

Yeah, He's very mysterious, but He can also be known, felt, and seen in the lives of followers of Christ. In fact, the main purpose of the Holy Spirit is "glorify Jesus" (John 16:14) by keeping us close to Him and performing His works on earth in and through us.

If you want a crash course in the Holy Spirit, spend the next few minutes reading John chapters 14-16. The coming of the Spirit is one of the greatest themes during Jesus' final meal on earth with His disciples.

Then continue reading Pete Battjes' new book *Holy Spirit Convergence* which you were wise enough to pick up. Pete is a guy who seems drenched in the Holy Spirit most of the time because he knows Him well and walks with Him.

That means that most of what Pete does brings honor and glory to Jesus. He and I first met at a large March for Jesus event in Seattle, Washington, where Pete was the guiding force. He was positive, upbeat, friendly, joyous, oozing faith and full of Someone who is extremely attractive.

The Holy Spirit.

Now Pete has written probably one of the most definitive books on the Holy Spirit that I have ever read. It will answer your questions from A-Z, and teach you about all aspects of the wonderful third member of the Triune God from Genesis to Revelation.

Being baptized in, as well as being filled with the Holy Spirit is a definite convergence of holiness and power in our lives and is marked by one thing.

Likeness.

Fullness is likeness.

If you are "filled" with God's Holy Spirit, then you will be like Him in His attributes, graces, humility, power, gifts, friendliness, and faith. Oh, yes, you will still be human and make mistakes. But God's Spirit inside of you will reveal Himself more and more as you are aware of Him, depend on Him, and seek to honor the Son.

Be filled with the Holy Spirit.

Be like Him.

So you can glorify Jesus.

Pete's book will help this blessed convergence take place in your life.

Dr. Ron Boehme
Youth With A Mission

9

Introduction

There is a reason you are reading this book right now.

The Lord Jesus Christ desires to give you greater revelation of Himself and His divine work. He wants you to be encouraged and inspired as you encounter Him in a fresh new way through the work of the Holy Spirit.

A Scripture that has ignited passion in me over the years is Zechariah 4:6,

> *"Then he said to me, 'This is the word of the LORD to Zerubbabel saying, 'Not by might nor by power, but by My Spirit,' says the LORD of hosts."*

This is the word of the LORD to you also.

The LORD of hosts calls each of us to trust Him and fulfill His purposes during our lifetime. They may not be of the same magnitude that Zerubbabel faced, but God's assignments are all significant.

He empowers us by the Holy Spirit in the process.

He continues to bring forth revelation by the Holy Spirit to instruct and guide His people, but not everyone is seeking, open, teachable, or obedient.

My prayer for you is that you will seek the revelation God has for you and that this book will enlarge your spiritual understanding in a greater way than you have experienced before.

You are part of His divine plan!

The Holy Spirit wants to keep revealing the will and ways of God to you. Some have not pursued the Lord and His continuing revelation from the Holy Spirit and have become weary, weak, and even confused.

I am confident you will be significantly changed as you follow along through the chapters of this book and see the hand of God working in the past and up to the present.

It is a great privilege to be Jesus' servant, to hear His voice, and follow where He leads through the work of the Holy Spirit.

The mysterious work of God through the Holy Spirit is marvelous. It is exciting. It is edifying. It is encouraging.

It is an on-going discovery and adventure that not only stretches the true believer's faith, but also brings great joy, peace, and power as the will of God is fulfilled for His glory.

In this book, you will discover the revelation of God's Word regarding the Person and ministry of the Holy Spirit. It will be enlightening and empowering.

Use it as a discipleship manual for personal growth, as well as to teach and train others.

I have chosen to use the New American Standard Bible (NASB) because of its' accuracy of interpretation and all personal pronouns are capitalized when pertaining to God. I believe this is both honoring to God and clarifying to the reader.

Are you ready? Let the discovery begin!

Chapter 1 – Understanding Convergence

Convergence is a fascinating reality that happens continually in our world on many different levels – naturally, relationally, and spiritually. Noah Webster, in his 1828 Dictionary, defines convergence as, "The quality of converging; tendency to one point."

Converging involves joining together, uniting, or merging together. This is illustrated in a natural way when two rivers merge or join together and become one. We have convergence relationally in marriage, as God reveals in Genesis 2:24, *"...and they shall become one flesh."*. The Lord joined the man and the woman together into a state of convergence.

Then, most significantly, there is the distinct spiritual convergence of God's divine intervention and joining with a true believer in Christ through the Holy Spirit.

Through the Holy Spirit, we experience an initial convergence into a relationship with Jesus through faith and emerge a different person.

We are united or joined with Christ. We have a divine encounter that impacts us for eternity as we yield to the drawing of the Holy Spirit.

The convergence of the Holy Spirit with our spirit brings about the transformation resulting in the spiritual new birth. Jesus explained this very thing to the Jewish religious leader, Nicodemus, who was searching for the way of eternal life. Jesus told him, *"...Truly, truly, I say to you, unless one is born of water and the Spirit, he cannot enter into the kingdom of God."* (John 3:5).

The Holy Spirit joins with a person's spirit, the eternal part of us. This convergence ushers a person into the kingdom of God, because they are born-again spiritually through the Holy Spirit.

People may have the *revelation* of God brought to them, but until there is the *illumination* of the Holy Spirit, there will be no spiritual *transformation*!

The Holy Spirit is the convergence of God with individuals, doing the will of the Father and the Son.

The Spirit is also the means to the building of Jesus' Church worldwide. We converge or unite with Christ's body, the Church, through the intervention of the Holy Spirit. This is an amazing part of the initial convergence experience.

He is the Person who unifies believers, binding them together in Christ and joining them to their forever family.

We should continually celebrate His incredible divine work in us and among us!

The Point of Decision

My initial Holy Spirit convergence experience happened at age sixteen in 1970. Growing up in Southern California, I was exposed to the Hippie movement of the 60's with "Love-Ins" on the beaches. I had been raised in a solid Christian home, attended Christian schools, and went to church twice every Sunday. I knew my catechism lessons, but I did not know Jesus. I knew all about Him and the truths of the Bible, but had not truly believed and surrendered my life to Him.

It was during a chapel service at the annual "Spiritual Emphasis Week" at Maranatha High School in San Gabriel, California, that I heard the testimony of several "Jesus People". They had been in the Hippie movement and still looked like Hippies. I inwardly laughed when I saw them. After the last one shared what Jesus meant to him and how his life had been changed by the power of God, I heard the Holy Spirit say to me – "They have what you need!" It wasn't an audible voice, but it came through loud and clear to me.

After the chapel, I went up to where these Jesus People were talking with some of my classmates. I stood back but wanted to hear more of what they had to say. I listened and then left to go to my next class. I just shrugged off all the "Jesus talk". This was the Tuesday chapel service of that week.

During the Friday chapel time, there were several students from Azusa Pacific University that came to share for the final day. The leader got up and announced they were not going to share their faith in Christ because others that week already had. Instead they were going to ask anyone who wanted to make a decision for Christ to stand up and do it.

Again, I heard the Holy Spirit speaking to me, but this time He said – "If you die today, you will go to Hell!" This really struck me! This was a "Come to Jesus" point of decision for me.

I froze in my seat, in shock of what I had just heard the Holy Spirit say. I had wanted to control my own life and do what appealed to me. I wanted the future to be "my" future. But, this was a clear point of decision making, one that had an eternal consequence. It was a clear call to trust and follow Christ.

I found myself standing. I looked at all my classmates in the room and declared – "Today I'm putting my faith in Jesus Christ and trusting Him for the rest of my life and I'm not turning back."

It was a true Holy Spirit convergence experience for me. I quit resisting the Holy Spirit and yielded to the truth that unless I surrendered my life to God and put my faith in Jesus as Savior and Lord, I would be eternally lost.

All that I had been taught growing up as a child took on new meaning because now I was born-again by the Holy Spirit through faith in Jesus. The *revelation* of truth with the *illumination* of the Holy Spirit brought the genuine inner spiritual *transformation*. I was forever changed.

Life was not the same after that day. I discovered that having Jesus in control of my life and trusting Him to lead me in the way that He desires is the best way to live.

This was my initial experience of Holy Spirit convergence. All true believers in Jesus have an initial convergence experience, in which they are born-again unto salvation. For some it may be less dramatic, such as praying with someone or on your own. Possibly going forward at an invitation during a worship service, at an evangelistic meeting or responding to a television or radio message. For others it may be more dramatic, but each experience is spiritually impacting.

Next, I want to share an example of the on-going convergence of the Holy Spirit. It is an illustration of the intervention of God in a Christ-follower's life.

This incident happened while my wife, Vivian, and I were completing our Crossroads Discipleship Training School (CDTS) with Youth With A Mission (YWAM) in Thailand during the Spring of 2001. The Holy Spirit intervened in an unusual way...

Give Him the Knife!

The witchdoctor had controlled the lives of the villagers for many years. He had spiritual power that caused the people to fear him and what he could do. Our YWAM team had been in this remote village in the mountains of Thailand for almost a week. To get to this village, our team of thirteen had to hike over three mountains and cross several rivers on foot with all our provisions.

When we arrived on the first day, just before the sun went down, we encountered fourteen huts, built up on stilts with animals walking around as they pleased. Other YWAM teams had come before us, but I sensed the greater work was yet to happen to bring the kingdom of God here.

The Thai pastor from another village who accompanied us had been encouraged by the work our team had accomplished. In just a matter of days we had put in the foundation of a new school building.

As the team leader, I was pondering one night about the assignment the Lord had given us and wondered what the final two days would hold. As I lay awake thinking, the Holy Spirit spoke into my mind, "Give him the knife!". He then revealed that the person to give it to was the elderly village witchdoctor.

I knew distinctly which knife I was to give away, for I had taken only one with me. It was a special jackknife I had purchased in the United States prior to coming to Thailand. It was for use on the two YWAM Outreaches I would be involved in, one here and the other in the Philippines. It was a knife I treasured and thought I would need over the next two months.

Now, the Holy Spirit was saying to give it up. Why this knife and not something else? I came under conviction that I needed to let go of the knife and give it to the witchdoctor as a gift. It was a gift the Holy Spirit wanted to use to somehow touch his heart.

The next day I consulted with the native pastor about being able to meet with the witchdoctor before leaving the following day, to present him with a gift. He later approached the elderly man who controlled the village and came back with the news that not only I, but the whole team was invited to come to his house that very afternoon. The opportunity now took on greater significance as exceptional favor was given to us.

I then shared with the team what the Holy Spirit had revealed to me and we spent time in prayer together before going. As the team approached the witchdoctor's house, which was elevated above the other dwellings on the far end of the village, we saw the man and his wife sitting on the deck waiting outside. I also was prompted by the Holy Spirit to bring a small bottle of anointing oil along to this meeting and apply it as I felt led.

The Thai pastor greeted the elderly man and his wife and introduced our team. Obviously, he had been observing our team interacting among his people and working hard on the hill opposite his dwelling.

He must have heard the sound when I blew the shofar (a ram's horn from Israel) each day, as well as, our songs of praise each morning and evening as we gathered together for worship. He must have been curious. It's quite possible that he had not personally met with anyone from the prior YWAM teams. This may have been a first encounter with foreigners.

After greeting the couple, I asked permission to present the gift of the jackknife. As he received it, he held it up and turned it over and over in his hands. I sensed that he recognized it as an object of worth. Most likely, he had never received a gift from the foreigners who had started coming to his village to work and share about a God named Jesus. I then asked if we could sing. When asked by the native pastor, he nodded in approval and we lifted our praise to the Lord Jesus, singing several songs as the Holy Spirit led us.

Before we left, I asked if we could pray for him and his wife. The pastor again made the request and it was granted. Different people on the team led out in prayer, specifically asking that salvation would come to this couple and the other villagers. We prayed the name and blood of Jesus over this leader and his family.

We left their dwelling that afternoon with great joy, knowing that the Holy Spirit had done a work that would one day bring glory to God.

I'm sure the word spread throughout the village of what was taking place. The people must have wondered what was going to happen as these foreigners went to meet with their spiritual leader. We left the village the next day knowing that our part of God's assignment had been completed.

It was six years later that the Thai pastor from Chang Mai, who we had initially worked with, sent me an email with a video attached. The video was entitled, "The Shaman's Redemption". It was about the very same witch-doctor, the village shaman, who we had reached out to. He had come to faith in Jesus Christ, along with his wife!

The video showed the villagers dancing for joy as his testimony was shared and also the evil spirit houses or altars being burned up. It also showed that the building we began to construct was complete and was being used as a school and a place of Christian worship on Sundays. Glory to God!

The Lord did His work among these very remote and primitive people, using something as simple as the gift of a jackknife, along with prayer and praise, to open the heart of a man who had been part of the kingdom of darkness all of his life.

This is an amazing witness of Holy Spirit convergence in a unique setting. As the Holy Spirit directed and obedience followed, the divine work of God transpired.

It is wonderful what can happen when a Christ-follower is open and obedient to the leading of the Holy Spirit.

Chapter 2 – Knowing the Holy Spirit

Some of those reading this have been raised in a church where the only exposure to the Holy Spirit has been in reciting The Apostle's Creed or a sermon on Pentecost Sunday. That was my experience until many years into adulthood.

Others may have received more teaching and have a greater knowledge or understanding of Him.

Before you continue, I'd like to challenge you to spend just two minutes and do a simple exercise.

Take time right now to write down what you know about the Holy Spirit in the space below.

The Holy Spirit Revealed

Where do we first encounter the Holy Spirit in Scripture? He is revealed in the book of "beginnings", Genesis. Many would readily point to Genesis 1:2, which states, *"...and the Spirit of God was moving over the surface of the waters."* But, the Holy Spirit is actually revealed in the very first verse of Scripture, *"In the beginning God..."* (Genesis 1:1).

He is God! He has Divine attributes as God, like the Father and the Son. The Old Testament Hebrew word for "Spirit" is *"ruwach"* (Genesis 1:2). [1] The New Testament Greek word is *"pneuma"* (Matthew 1:18). [2]

Both the Hebrew and Greek words can be translated as "breath, spirit, life, wind" as well as, "breath of life".

Here are several foundational attributes that must be acknowledged pertaining to the Holy Spirit. More will be discussed later.

- He is *Eternal* (Hebrews 9:14). This identifies Him as having no beginning and no end. He was not created, the same as the Father and the Son.

- He is *Omnipresent* (Psalm 139:7-8). This identifies Him as being present everywhere.

- He is *Omnipotent* (Luke 1:35). This identifies Him as being all-powerful.

- He is *Omniscient* (I Corinthians 2:10-11). This identifies Him as being all-knowing.

Scripture reveals that Almighty God consists of three Persons, Who are one God. They are distinct, yet equal Persons, Who are inseparable and indivisibly One God.

Each Person is identified clearly as Father, Son, and Holy Spirit, both in the Old and New Testament. It is essential to acknowledge this truth in our understanding of God and His relationship with us.

This mysterious reality of God may be known as the "God-Head" or "Trinity". These three Persons are Creator, Sustainer, and Sovereign Ruler of the universe. They are in complete unity, but have different roles.

The God-Head functions as co-eternal, co-existent, and co-equal, in a completely unified relationship.

Unfortunately, there are those in the realm of Christianity who do not hold to this revelation of God, therefore it must be established clearly.

How do we know God is more than one Person? How do we know there are not three separate Gods?

- **Genesis1:1 – *"In the beginning <u>God</u> created..."***

The Hebrew interpretation for God in this text is Elohim. It is a plural noun, which clearly identifies God as being more than one Person.

- **Genesis 1:26** – *"Then God said, 'Let <u>Us</u> make man in <u>Our</u> image, according to <u>Our</u> likeness…"*

Here, plural pronouns are used to clarify that more than one Person is identified as God.

- **Genesis 11:7** – *"Come, let <u>Us</u> go down and there confuse their language, so that they will not understand one another's speech."*

Again, when God intervened at the Tower of Babel, the plural pronoun is used to identify that more than one Person is acting.

- **Deuteronomy 6:4** – *"Hear, O Israel! The LORD is our God, the LORD is one!"*

We must recognize that the LORD our God is one. There is one God, Who consists of three Divine Persons.

- **John 1:1-2** – *"In the beginning was the Word, and the Word was with God, and the Word was God. He was in the beginning with God."*

This Scripture firmly establishes Jesus, the Word, as being *"with God"*, as well as being *"God"*. There are multiple Persons represented in the Godhead.

- **Matthew 3:16-17** – *"After being baptized, Jesus came up immediately from the water; and behold, the heavens were opened, and he saw the Spirit of God descending as a dove and lighting on Him, and behold, a voice out of the heavens, said, 'This is My beloved Son, in whom I am well-pleased.' "*

Clearly, we have all three Persons of the God-head represented and acknowledged distinctly when Jesus was baptized in the Jordan River by John the Baptizer.

- **John 17:22** – *"The glory which You have given Me I have given to them; that they may be one, just as We are one;"*

Jesus reveals in His prayer the reality of being "one" with the Father, thus identifying Himself as God, along with the Father.

- **Matthew 28:19** – *"Go therefore and make disciples of all the nations, baptizing them in the name of the Father and the Son and the Holy Spirit,"*

Jesus revealed and affirmed the three Persons of the God-head in His final instructions before He ascended back to Heaven. He wants His followers to accept Who the living and true God is.

The Holy Spirit is one Person of the Godhead. The Father and the Son, Jesus Christ, are the other two.

The God-Connection

In our understanding of Who God is, we shouldn't miss what I call the "God-connection" that is evident in Scripture.

It is crucial to recognize that the Father, Son, and Holy Spirit are "inter-dependent", not independent. They are continually interacting together and cooperating with each other in complete unity, after all, they are ONE.

There are three main areas where we see evidence of this "inter-dependence" among the Godhead:

- **Creation** – Genesis 1:1-2, 26; Hebrews 1:1-2, 10.

  All three Persons take part in the creation of the universe, the earth, and mankind.

- **Redemption** – Isaiah 63:8-16; I Peter 1:2.

  All three Persons are involved in the saving work of redeeming humanity.

- **Sanctification** – John 14:26, 15:26; Romans 8:26-30.

All three Persons are working for our good in the process of sanctification.

The Father, Son, and Holy Spirit accomplish the supernatural work together, each with a distinct role and responsibility in fulfilling their divine purposes through inter-dependence.

Take time to look up the Scriptures identified and see the evidence of the "God-connection". It will increase your knowledge and understanding of the ways and work of God in your own life.

Distinct Names of the Holy Spirit

In the former exercise of writing down what you knew about the Holy Spirit, you may have identified a number of His names.

Here are some of His specific names revealed to us in Scripture. I was amazed at the many different titles the Holy Spirit is identified by, you may be also. I'd encourage you to say each one aloud as you read it.

1. **Spirit of God** (Genesis 1:2; Romans 8:9,14)

2. **Spirit of Christ** (Romans 8:9)

3. **Comforter** (John 16:7 KJV)

4. **Holy Spirit** (Luke 1:35; John 14:26; Hebrews 10:15)

5. **Spirit of His Son** (Galatians 4:6)

6. **Spirit of truth** (John 14:17; 15:26; 16:13)

7. **Spirit of grace** (Hebrews 10:29)

8. **Spirit of life** (Romans 8:2)

9. **Spirit of adoption** (Romans 8:15 ESV)

10. **Spirit of sonship** (Rom. 8:15 NIV)

11. **Counselor** (John 14:16; 15:26 NIV)

12. **Spirit of the Lord** (Isaiah 61:1; Luke 4:18)

13. **Helper** (John 14:16; 15:26; 16:7)

14. **Spirit of Him** (the Father) (Romans 8:11)

15. **Spirit** (Luke 4:14; Acts 11:12; Romans 8:5; Galatians 5:25)

16. **Spirit of your Father** (Matthew 10:20)

17. **Spirit of holiness** (Romans 1:4 NIV, ESV)

18. **Holy Spirit of promise** (Ephesians 1:13)

19. **Spirit of Jesus** (Acts 16:7)

20. **Spirit of glory and of God** (I Peter 4:14)

21. **Spirit of wisdom and revelation** (Ephesians 1:17 NIV)

22. **Spirit of Jesus Christ** (Philippians 1:19)

Each name reveals how great the Holy Spirit is as God. Each name helps us identify how significant He is to the believer.   Each name is referring to the same Person, known most often as the Holy Spirit.

I am so thankful that Jesus clarifies any confusion that may occur regarding Who the Holy Spirit is. He reveals to His followers, that they have *"another Counselor"* (John14:16 NIV).

Jesus is truly the *"Wonderful Counselor"* (Isaiah 9:6 NIV) as the promised Messiah. But, the Holy Spirit is the other *"Counselor"*, Who will fulfill Jesus' work in the world until He returns in glory.

Jesus is talking about the Holy Spirit as our personal Comforter, Counselor, or Helper. The Greek word is "Parakletos", with the literal meaning of, "called to one's side" or "to one's aid".[1]

We are given an Advocate, Consoler, and Comforter from the Father and the Son. He is the One who will "come along side" us as we follow Jesus. We need His help to guide us daily and open up the revelation of God's Word to us continually.

This should greatly encourage us, knowing that Jesus is working in us through the Holy Spirit. We can call on Him any time. The many references given in Scripture regarding the Holy Spirit affirm to us God's divine work on our behalf.

Are you up for a real challenge? Make it a goal to underline or highlight every reference or mention of God's Spirit in the Bible. You will be truly amazed at how prominent He is!

Manifestations of the Holy Spirit

People are often confused about the Holy Spirit because He manifests Himself in a variety of ways. Some are beyond our understanding. He can operate in some mysterious ways, which surprises certain people and may even frighten others. Let's look at His distinct manifestations in Scripture that will enlighten us.

1. **Hovering:** This manifestation took place at the creation of the earth (Genesis 1:2 NIV, ESV). This is also translated as *"moving over the surface"*. We don't know specifically what this entailed but it was effective in the formation of the earth. The

Holy Spirit was very active in creation from the beginning.

2. **Prophesying:** In the Old Testament, this manifestation involved the seventy Israelite Elders (Numbers 11:16-17; 24-30); the anointing of Saul as king by Samuel (I Samuel 10:5-11); the situation regarding King Saul's soldiers who were sent to capture David (I Samuel 19:20-23).

    In the New Testament, this manifestation is evident with the disciples in Ephesus (Acts 19:1-6); Philip's four daughters (Acts 21:9 ESV, NKJV); Agabus (Acts 21:10-11, Acts 11:27-28); among the Antioch believers (Acts 13:2); the Apostle Paul's teaching (I Corinthians 13:9, 14:1-5).

3. **Supernatural Conception:** This manifestation took place with the incarnation of Jesus Christ, the Son of God. The angel Gabriel revealed the miraculous work of God through the divine work of the Holy Spirit in Mary, a virgin. (Matthew 1:18, 20; Luke 1:35).

4. **Christ's Resurrection:** This manifestation took place after Jesus died and was buried, but arose on the third day. Peter relates the work of the Holy Spirit in connection with Jesus' resurrection in I Peter 3:18. Paul also identifies this divine action and the involvement of the **"Spirit of holiness"**

(Romans 1:4 NIV, ESV), as well as the **"Spirit of Him who raised Christ Jesus from the dead."** (Romans 8:11).

5. **The Form of a Dove:** This manifestation took place just after Jesus was baptized by John the Baptizer and was visible to those present (Matthew 3:16; Luke 3:22; John 1:32).

6. **A Noise like a Violent, Rushing Wind:** This manifestation took place on the Day of Pentecost in Jerusalem (Acts 2:2). It was very noticeable and drew people who were in Jerusalem to where the 120 believers were joined in prayer.

7. **Tongues of fire:** This manifestation took place on the Day of Pentecost in Jerusalem upon the 120 believers gathered together (Acts 2:3).

8. **Speaking in other tongues:** This manifestation took place on the Day of Pentecost upon the 120 believers gathered together (Acts 2:4).

9. **Supernatural shaking:** This manifestation took place while the early believers were praying in a specific house (Acts 4:31).

10. **Speaking with tongues:** This manifestation took place on numerous occasions in the expansion of

the Church beginning with Pentecost. The next instance was regarding the Gentile converts in the home of Cornelius, the Roman Centurion (Acts 10:44-46, 11:15-17).

Then again, in Ephesus, when Paul laid his hands on the believers after being water baptized. This is the fulfillment of Jesus' prophecy in Mark 16:17. This is a manifestation that only comes after believing in Christ and is the work of the Holy Spirit for the glory of God.

11. **Being Filled with the Holy Spirit:** This manifestation is revealed among believers on various occasions (Acts 2:4; 4:31; 9:17). The Apostle Paul gives instruction on this in Ephesians 5:18.

As a person examines each of these unique manifestations you many come to the conclusion that I have -- the Holy Spirit is unpredictable! This is a challenge to many people, and some have reacted in fear to what they do not understand about the Holy Spirit.

Others have tried to limit the work of the Holy Spirit, which I consider a very dangerous thing to do. No one should assume to know all about God and His ways. When the Holy Spirit reveals Himself in whatever manifestation He chooses, we can be assured that He is working for our good and God's glory.

Always know that the Holy Spirit will not act in a manner that will contradict God's Word which He inspired.

We can trust Him to be doing the work of Jesus in our lives when we are yielded to Him by being open and teachable. Remember, as God, He can manifest as He chooses to fulfill the purposes of God.

The Glory Room

For a number of years a small group of men in Snoqualmie, Washington, have been meeting weekly in a space referred to as, "The Upper Room". The focus of sharing personal needs and praying for each other shifted to focusing on the Holy Spirit and His work among them.

Now, as these men gather together, they expect the Holy Spirit to reveal specific matters and move in their midst. They invite the Holy Spirit to come and work His work. As a result, the place of meeting is now identified as "The Glory Room", because of the divine work taking place.

An important aspect often left out of our lives is being still in God's Presence. It's great to share needs and we all have them, but it is crucial to allow the Holy Spirit to bring revelation. Psalm 46:10 (NIV) calls us to *"Be still, and know that I am God…"*. God, the Holy Spirit, looks for opportunities to reveal matters of importance, but many times we are not allowing Him.

On one occasion in "The Glory Room", the Holy Spirit revealed that for those of us who were married, we were to go home that evening, look our wife in the eyes and say from our heart, "May Jesus bless you." Does that sound odd? To some it may, but to those gathered there that night, it was an encouragement to do what pleases God. Our spouse needs to hear us bless them. Some of the men there may have never done anything like that before, but we all knew it was a "God-thing".

Another evening, we were prompted by the Spirit to be aware of someone in crisis who we would encounter in the days ahead. When we connect with them, we were given the challenge to encourage them with the words, "Jesus loves you and cares about you." A number of us shared a week later specific "divine contacts" where this was done. The Holy Spirit was preparing us for what was to come.

Each time the group meets, the evening ends with one of the men serving The Lord's Supper. At times, as he is serving the elements, the Holy Spirit will put a word or message of encouragement on his heart for someone. He will then speak the blessing to that person, as the Spirit leads him. It is glorious!

These men also meet once a month on a Saturday at a park overlooking the Snoqualmie Valley. It is a high place where they pray over the pastors, churches, and people residing in the valley. The time is concluded by partaking of The Lord's Supper in the beauty of God's creation. It has an impact on those who faithfully gather each month and over the spiritual realm of the region. It is a convergence experience where the Holy Spirit leads those gathered in Jesus' name.

These are just a few of the unique workings of God in our midst – they are life-changing because they edify and affirm God's work among us for His glory and our good.

Again the key is openness to whatever the Holy Spirit desires to do, whenever He desires to do it, and however He desires to do it. We should want His agenda when we meet and be willing to adjust accordingly so He can work.

We must be discerning and sensitive to how He would lift up Jesus and edify the body of believers in each situation.

Chapter 3 – The Impact of the Holy Spirit in the Old Testament

Many people are unaware of the incredible impact that the Holy Spirit had on certain people and situations in the Old Testament.

Often pastors and teachers will focus only on the work of the Holy Spirit after His manifestation on Pentecost. I believe much is lost by not acknowledging His involvement from the beginning of creation. This is foundational.

In the Old Testament, there are over 70 times that the Holy Spirit, Spirit of God, Spirit of the Lord, or Spirit are mentioned. He is a significant Person in the Old Testament.

The following Scriptures are a few among many that demonstrate the Spirit's significance among humanity prior to the coming of Christ at His incarnation.

Take time to reflect on each situation and marvel at the direct intervention of God. Remember, the Holy Spirit operates in ways that are higher than our ways for a distinct purpose. Some of these convergence experiences are very unusual!

- **Genesis 1:2** – *"...and the <u>Spirit of God</u> was moving over the surface of the waters."*

As mentioned previously, this is regarding the creation of the earth. He was operating in a unique and creative manner to determine and design the beauty that we behold today.

- **Genesis 6:3** – *"Then the LORD said, 'My <u>Spirit</u> shall not strive with man forever..."*

This is regarding the evil on the earth during the time of Noah and God's decision to destroy the world with a flood.

- **Exodus 31:2-3** – *"See, I have called by name Bezalel...I have filled him with the <u>Spirit of God</u> in wisdom, in understanding, in knowledge, and in all kinds of craftsmanship..."*

This is regarding the building of the Tabernacle and the items inside it that were to be used for worship.

- **Numbers 11:17** – *"Then I will come down and speak with you there, and I will take of the <u>Spirit</u> who is upon you, and will put Him upon them; and they shalll bear the burden of the people with you, so that you will not bear it alone."*

This is regarding the appointment of seventy elders to serve the Israelites under Moses and relieve him of the great responsibility of judging and counseling all the people of Israel after being delivered from Egypt.

- **I Samuel 10:6** – *"Then the <u>Spirit of the LORD</u> will come upon you mightily, and you shall prophesy with them and be changed into another man."*

This is regarding the prophet Samuel anointing Saul as the first king of Israel and how God would confirm the appointment as king. This action designated Saul as the true successor of the judges of Israel.

- **I Samuel 19:20** – *"Then Saul sent messengers to take David, but when they saw the company of the prophets prophesying, with Samuel standing and presiding over them, the <u>Spirit of God</u> came upon the messengers of Saul; and they also prophesied."*

This is regarding King Saul trying to capture David due to his jealousy of him, but the Holy Spirit intervened and the soldiers were changed.

- **I Samuel 19:23-24** – *"He proceeded to Naioth in Ramah; and the <u>Spirit of God</u> came upon him also, so that he went along prophesying...He also stripped off his clothes, and he too prophesied* *before Samuel and lay down naked all that day and all that night..."*

This is regarding King Saul trying to do what his soldiers were unable to do in capturing David. Again, the Holy Spirit changed things dramatically and humbled this prideful king.

■ **II Samuel 23:2** – *"The <u>Spirit of the Lord</u> spoke by me,*
  And His word was on my tongue."

This is regarding the divine anointing of the Holy Spirit to speak through God's servant, King David. These were some of the last words he spoke, put into a song.

■ **II Chronicles 20:14-15** – *"Then in the midst of the assembly the <u>Spirit of the LORD</u> came upon Jahaziel...and he said...thus says the LORD to you, 'Do not fear or be dismayed because of this great multitude, for the battle is not yours but God's.' "*

This is regarding the intervention of the Lord on behalf of King Jehoshaphat and the people of Judah to destroy the enemies coming against them. It was a specific prophecy given to Jahaziel to speak forth by the Spirit.

- **Nehemiah 9:20** – *"You gave Your good <u>Spirit</u> to instruct them…"*

This is regarding the prayer the Levites lifted up to God in repentance on behalf of the Israelites. They were acknowledging God's divine work and faithfulness among them in the wilderness through the Holy Spirit.

- **Job 33:4** – *"The <u>Spirit of God</u> has made me, And the breath of the Almighty gives me life."*

This is regarding the advice given to Job by his friend Elihu during Job's intense season of suffering.

- **Psalm 51:11** – *"Do not cast me away from Your presence, And do not take Your <u>Holy Spirit</u> from me."*

This is regarding King David confessing his sin to God and seeking His mercy and forgiveness. He became fully aware of the consequences of his sin against God, himself, and others.

- **Psalm 139:7** – *"Where can I go from Your <u>Spirit</u>? Or where can I flee from Your presence?"*

This is regarding David revealing the truth about God being everywhere present. As God, the Holy Spirit is omnipresent. A truth that our finite minds can not comprehend, but we know to be true by faith.

- **Isaiah 11: 2** (NIV, ESV, NKJV) – *"The <u>Spirit of the LORD</u> will rest on Him,*
  The <u>Spirit</u> of wisdom and understanding,
  The <u>Spirit</u> of counsel and strength,
  The <u>Spirit</u> of knowledge and the fear of the LORD."

This prophecy is regarding the anointing of the future Messiah who was to come.

These are attributes of Christ imparted through the Holy Spirit. They were all evident in Jesus during His life and ministry.

The same Holy Spirit imparts this anointing to believers today who are receptive and yielded to Him.

- **Isaiah 59:21** – *"And as for Me, this is My covenant with them, says the LORD: My <u>Spirit</u> which is upon you, and My words which I have put in your mouth, shall not depart from your mouth, nor from the mouth of your offspring, nor from the mouth of your offspring's offspring, says the LORD, from now and forever."*

This is regarding God's promise to His people to be faithful to His covenant. God's revelation will continue through the generations and will result in a Redeemer. God continues to give His people hope.

- **Isaiah 61:1** – *"The <u>Spirit of the Lord GOD</u> is upon me,*
  Because the LORD has anointed me…"

This also is regarding the anointing of the future Messiah who was to come. Jesus claimed this prophecy about Himself during His ministry (see Luke 4:18-19, 21). He fulfilled this role as the Son of God through the anointing of the Holy Spirit. The four Gospels reveal the reality of Who Jesus is and the manifestation of the Spirit's power.

- **Isaiah 63:10-11** – *"But they rebelled*
  And grieved His <u>Holy Spirit</u>;
  Therefore He turned Himself to become their enemy,
  He fought against them…Where is He who put His <u>Holy Spirit</u> in the midst of them…"

This is regarding a time of Israel's turning away from God by rebelling against the Holy Spirit. God allowed His people to be taken captive and they experienced great suffering as a result of their choice. It is a serious thing to grieve the Spirit and turn away from the Lord with a stubborn and unrepentant heart.

- **Ezekiel 2:2** – *"As He spoke to me the Spirit entered me and set me on my feet; and I heard Him speaking to me."*

This is regarding the prophet being called by God to warn the rebellious Israelites. He was very much aware of the Holy Spirit moving upon him and speaking into his heart. He was yielded and obedient to the challenging call given him and empowered by the Holy Spirit to fulfill God's work.

- **Ezekiel 3:12, 14, 24** – *"Then the Spirit lifted me up, and I heard a great rumbling sound behind me, 'Blessed be the glory of the LORD in His place...So the Spirit lifted me up and took me away...The Spirit then entered me and made me stand on my feet, and He spoke with me..."*

This is regarding the prophet's commissioning by God and the intervention of the Holy Spirit. Something supernatural occurred, similar to Philip the Evangelist (see Acts 8:39). There appears to be a divine "translation" from one place to another through the Spirit of God. God Almighty is the God of the supernatural!

- **Joel 2:28-29** – *"It will come about after this That I will pour out My Spirit on all mankind... Even on the male and female servants I will pour out My Spirit in those days."*

This is regarding the coming work of God through the Holy Spirit after Christ's ascension back to heaven. This happened on Pentecost. The prophet Joel was revealing the great plan of God to reach all people with salvation. The impact of this unique outpouring of the Spirit on all mankind would result in people receiving God's revelation through prophesy, dreams, and visions. The purpose being, *"...that whoever calls on the name of the LORD will be delivered..."* (Joel 2:32). God is calling all people to call upon Him for eternal salvation.

■ **Zechariah 4:6 –** *"Then he said to me, 'This is the word of the LORD to Zerubbabel saying, Not by might nor by power, but by My Spirit, says the LORD of hosts.' "*

This is regarding God calling Zerubbabel to complete the work of rebuilding the temple and giving him the assurance of the Spirit's enablement in the process.

God can use people if they rely on Him and allow the Spirit to do what only the Spirit can do. Nothing has changed regarding this truth in the work of God's kingdom. Christ-followers must humble themselves and seek the power of the Spirit in all they do.

These are amazing interventions and revelations that lead into the continuing work of the Holy Spirit in the New Testament. Each one speaks to us of the Spirit's unique role in the plan of God for humanity.

But, this is not all we discover in the Old Testament regarding the convergence of the Holy Spirit. He also was the One who imparted an "anointing" of God for specific assignments on specific people at a specific time.

The Old Testament "Anointer"

Take a look at this list of individuals who experienced God's power through the Holy Spirit. These are ordinary people like each one of us. God can use anyone at anytime if they are open and obedient to His leading and power.

We discover a unique convergence of God's Spirit with these individuals for the glory of God.

1. **Joseph** (Genesis 41:38)

2. **Bezalel** (Exodus 31:2)

3. **Moses** (Numbers 11:17)

4. **Joshua** (Numbers 27:18)

5. **Othniel** (Judges 3:10)

6. **Gideon** (Judges 6:34)

7. **Jephthah** (Judges 11:29)

8. **Samson** (Judges 14:6, 19; 15:14-15)

9. **Saul** (I Samuel 10:10; 11:6)

10. **David** (I Samuel 16:13)

11. **Elijah** (I Kings 8:12; II Kings 2:16)

12. **Elisha** (II Kings 2:15)

13. **Amasai** (I Chronicles 12:18)

14. **Azariah** (II Chronicles 15:1)

15. **Jahaziel** (II Chronicles 20:14)

16. **Zechariah** (II Chronicles 24:20)

17. **Ezekiel** (Ezekiel 2:2)

18. **Daniel** (Daniel 4:9; 5:11; 6:3)

19. **Micah** (Micah 3:8)

20. **Zerubbabel** (Zechariah 4:6)

The numerous references of the convergence of the Holy Spirit with specific individuals in the Old Testament are often overlooked, but they played a crucial role in revealing the work of God through the ages. These are history-makers!

These individuals all played a significant part in God's plan for His people and His eternal purposes. They are recorded to be an inspiration to us. They are also an example to us, to encourage us in the work Jesus has called us to in our life. You can call upon the Holy Spirit no matter what your challenge may be, He is available.

We Really Need This!

I believe it is important for us to take a closer look at what is revealed in Isaiah 11:2-3 (NIV) and see how it applies to Christ-followers.

We discover a number of distinct attributes of the Holy Spirit's anointing that would come upon the Messiah. As already mentioned, Jesus gave evidence of these in His life and ministry. These are identified as:

- **The Spirit of wisdom and understanding.**

- **The Spirit of counsel and power.**

- **The Spirit of knowledge and of the fear of the LORD.**

We must remember that the same Holy Spirit, Who imparted a unique anointing on Jesus for doing the will of the Father, indwells every true believer.

We need the Holy Spirit's anointing to operate as servants of Christ and fulfill His purposes in ministry. We need the following to live for God's glory: "wisdom... understanding...counsel...power...knowledge...the fear of the LORD".

Henry and Richard Blackaby share significant insight on how relevant just one aspect of this anointing is for a believer. In their daily devotional, <u>Experiencing God Day by Day</u>, they point out the following regarding "The Spirit of wisdom".

<u>The Spirit of Wisdom</u>

"The Spirit of the Lord shall rest upon Him, the Spirit of wisdom and understanding, the Spirit of counsel and might, the Spirit of knowledge and of the fear of the Lord." (Isaiah 11:2 NKJV)

"Throughout His ministry, Jesus relied upon the Holy Spirit to direct Him as He made crucial decisions and faced relentless opposition (Mark 1:12). Centuries earlier, Isaiah had described what the Spirit's presence would mean for the Savior. The Spirit would give Jesus the knowledge of the will and ways of the Father. As a young boy, Jesus already possessed unusual knowledge of God's Word (Luke 2:47). The Spirit enabled Jesus to take the Word of

God and apply it effectively to the specific needs of those He encountered.

If you are a Christian, the same Spirit abides in you. At times, you may pray and ask God to send His Spirit 'in power.' That is the only way the Spirit ever comes! More importantly, the Spirit will come in wisdom, bringing the understanding of God's ways.

You need God's wisdom for the decisions you face (Rom. 11:33). Perhaps God has placed you in a position of great responsibility, and you feel overwhelmed by the decisions you must make. It may be in your role as parent, or friend, or leader that you long for the wisdom of God. The same Spirit who enabled Jesus to see through the deceptions of Satan will also guide you through the temptations that confront you. Pray that God will fill you with His Spirit of wisdom so that through the decisions you make you can live your life effectively." [1]

Awesome insight! We do need to pray for God's Spirit of wisdom, as well as, understanding, counsel, might, knowledge, and the fear of the Lord. These attributes are each significant in living the abundant life Jesus came to give us (see John 10:10).

We have a Helper, sent to work in and through us. Don't hesitate to call upon Him each day.

Incredible Revelation

Very few people realize that all three Persons of the God-Head are identified clearly in the Old Testament. It is exciting to discover this revelation specifically in Isaiah 63. Take special note of the following verses:

> **Isaiah 63: 8-9** *"...So He became their <u>Savior</u>...*
> *And the <u>angel of His presence</u> saved them;*
> *In His love and in His mercy He redeemed*
> *them..."*

This is a reference to the Son of God or Pre-Incarnate Christ, the same as Exodus 23:20-23 and Joshua 5:13-6:2. This is a clear reference to the Person of the Son of God in the Old Testament.

> **Isaiah 63:10-11** *"...And grieved His <u>Holy</u>*
> *<u>Spirit</u>...Where is He who put His <u>Holy Spirit</u> in*
> *the midst of them..."*

This is a clear reference to the Person of the Holy Spirit in the Old Testament.

> **Isaiah 63:16** *"For You are our <u>Father</u>...You, O*
> *LORD, are our <u>Father</u>, our Redeemer from of*
> *old is Your name."*

This is a reference to the Person of the Father in the Old Testament.

This is significant evidence of the Holy Spirit being God and working in unity with the Father and the Son to accomplish the purpose of redeeming lost mankind.

This correlates with what is revealed in the New Testament regarding the God-Head and affirms the truth about God. Don't let anyone try to persuade you otherwise from this foundational revelation of God Himself in His Word.

Who's the Author?

The Bible is not one book. In reality it is 66 books compiled together! These 66 books have been composed over a span of many centuries, by 40 different writers. These writers are not the authors of the various books that comprise what we know as The Holy Bible.

There is only one Author – The Holy Spirit! He is the Author of both the Old and New Testament books. The following Scripture texts confirm this:

- **II Samuel 23:2 –** *"The Spirit of the Lord spoke by me,*
  And His word was on my tongue."

This was declared by King David. He wrote many of the Psalms, which were inspired by the Holy Spirit, as well as other portions of Scripture.

■ **Isaiah 59:21** – *As for Me, this is My covenant with them, says the LORD: My Spirit which is upon you, and My words which I have put in your mouth shall not depart from your mouth, nor from the mouth of your offspring..."*

There is a direct connection between the anointing of the Holy Spirit on Isaiah and the words given him to speak and later write. They are inspired words of truth from the Spirit.

■ **John 14:26** – *"But the Helper, the Holy Spirit, whom the Father will send in My name, He will teach you all things, and bring to your remembrance all that I said to you."*

Jesus confirms the Holy Spirit's work as Teacher and Author of what the disciples would record later. He inspired them and instructed them precisely what to write as the revelation of God. These writings took place many years after Jesus ascended back to Heaven and are in great detail. They could only have been reiterated by Divine inspiration.

■ **I Corinthians 2:12-13** – *"Now we have received, not the spirit of the world, but the Spirit who is from God, so that we may know the things freely given to us by God, which things we also speak, not in words taught by human wisdom, but in* *those taught by the Spirit, combining spiritual thoughts with spiritual words."*

When it comes to eternal truth and our salvation depends on it, we want what is of the Holy Spirit, not what is of some person's own wisdom or belief. The Apostle Paul makes it clear where the inspiration comes from – the Spirit.

Many in our world still look to human wisdom and are deceived – what a tragedy.

- **II Timothy 3:16** – *"All Scripture is inspired by God and profitable for teaching, for reproof, for correction, for training in righteousness;"*

The Holy Spirit is God. This inspiration of Scripture makes the Holy Spirit directly responsible for all that is written. He is the only Author.

- **II Peter 1:20-21** – *" But know this first of all, that no prophecy of Scripture is a matter of one's own interpretation, for no prophecy was ever made by an act of human will, but men moved by the Holy Spirit spoke from God."*

Clearly the Holy Spirit is the One revealing what was spoken and written by different men as writers. They were inspired so we can be confident of God's truth in Holy Scripture, which is the Bible.

- **Revelation 1:10-11** – *"I was in the Spirit on the Lord's day, and I heard behind me a loud voice like the sound of a trumpet, saying, 'Write in a book what you see..."*

The Apostle John, being *"in the Spirit"*, was the scribe. He was to write down what Jesus instructed him to write through the Spirit.

- **Revelation 2:7** – *"He who has an ear, let him hear what the Spirit says to the churches."*

Jesus was using the Holy Spirit to communicate His message to various churches. This statement regarding the Spirit is repeated after each letter of Jesus to the seven churches in Revelation 2-3. The involvement is clear of the Holy Spirit's role in the writing of the Book of Revelation.

As Christ-followers, we will be challenged by our culture regarding the validity of Scripture. We must stand firm on the revelation of Who the author is, and that Scripture is inerrant, inspired, infallible, and imparts God's unchangeable truths. These are God's absolutes!

In a society where the mindset is that everything is relative to the individual and circumstances, God's Word stands on the absolutes that have been established and are to be upheld by those who are true people of faith.

Again, the very fact that the four Gospels were written many years after Jesus' ascension, with the precise details of what Jesus said and what took place, confirms that only the Holy Spirit could impart this information to the writers. It's something I marvel at and thank God for.

The Bible is a miracle – it is God's divine work through the unique convergence of the Holy Spirit upon specific men.

We can rejoice in the truth of what has been given us through the Holy Spirit. He was at work then and is at work now in us, to help us believe and live out the revelation of God.

I am convinced that a person lives what they truly believe. How I live and what I say reveals what's in my heart. Actions do speak louder than words, right?

Each of our lives as Christ-followers, should reflect the truth of the Scriptures that we believe in. We need the Spirit's help to do this, just as the first disciples and early Christians did.

Chapter 4 – The Impact of the Holy Spirit in the New Testament

The Gospels reveal the continued work of the Holy Spirit in fulfilling the plan of God from the Old Covenant into the New Covenant. There are over 140 times that He is mentioned in the New Testament.

Something very unusual is foretold to a Jewish priest named Zacharias. He is told that his wife would conceive a son in her old age and he would have a very specific purpose in God's plan. This child was to be named John, and would *"...be filled with the Holy Spirit while yet in his mother womb...It is he who will go as a forerunner before Him in the spirit and power of Elijah..."* (Luke 1:15,17).

This child would be the fulfillment of the last prophecy given nearly 400 years earlier by the prophet Malachi – *"Behold, I am going to send you Elijah the prophet before the coming of the great and terrible day of the Lord."* (Malachi 4:5).

After the birth of John, the Holy Spirit does something unusual in his father – *"And his father Zacharias was filled with the Holy Spirit and prophesied..."* (Luke 1:67).

His prophecy brought glory to God because it resulted from a fresh filling with the Holy Spirit. This unusual anointing on both Zacharias and his unborn son are evidence of the continuing convergence of the Holy Spirit. He is actively working and joining with humanity to do the things of God. It should not surprise us that He does something so totally unexpected.

This convergence leads up to the most significant convergence of all history!

Matthew, the writer of the first Gospel, is inspired to declare what humanity has been earnestly waiting for, the coming of the Messiah. He would be Immanuel – *"God with us"*. Matthew reveals:

"Now the birth of Jesus Christ was as follows: when His mother Mary had been betrothed to Joseph, before they came together she was found to be with child by the Holy Spirit." (Matthew 1:18)

It was *"by the Holy Spirit"* that the Son of God entered humanity through a virgin woman named Mary. The Holy Spirit, being God, was the means through which Jesus Christ, the Son of God, would be conceived in Mary and remain sinless as God in the flesh. What a marvelous, miraculous convergence!

An angel of the Lord confirmed this very truth to Joseph also, whom Mary was engaged to. The angel stated:

"...Joseph, son of David, do not be afraid to take Mary as your wife; for the child who has been conceived in her is of the Holy Spirit." (Matthew 1:20).

There are Biblical scholars who believe the miracle of the Incarnation – God becoming man through the intervention of the Holy Spirit – is the greatest of all miracles.

This revelation given to the world changes all of history. The Wonder of wonders unfolds as the Holy Spirit does His work completely, and there can be no mistaking how it happened. God did what only God could do. Praise be to His name!

Jesus' Ministry in the Holy Spirit

The Gospel of Luke provides us with a clear understanding of the role of the Holy Spirit in the public ministry of Jesus. We discover seven significant matters that had an impact on Jesus and those He ministered to. We can view them as spiritual convergence matters.

1. **Anointing** – Luke 3:21-22a

   "Now when all the people were baptized, Jesus was also baptized, and while He was praying,

heaven opened, and the Holy Spirit descended upon Him in bodily form like a dove..."

The Holy Spirit came upon Jesus with a unique anointing as He began His public ministry at His baptism by John the Baptizer. This ushered Jesus into the next phase of His life whereby He would declare the kingdom of God and do the work of God leading up to His sacrifice on the cross. It was truly a divine convergence.

2. **Affirmation** – Luke 3:22b

...and a voice came out of heaven, 'You are My beloved Son, in You I am well pleased."

As the Holy Spirit descended upon Jesus, the Father audibly spoke and affirmed Jesus as the Son of God. No greater affirmation could be given by the Father than the words of affection and confirmation – *"You are My beloved Son, in You I am well-pleased."* This was a divine and sacred experience involving all three Persons of the Trinity.

3. **Filling** – Luke 4:1

"Jesus, full of the Holy Spirit, returned..."

Jesus received a special infilling when the Spirit descended upon Him after His baptism. This points us to what will occur later at Pentecost when the 120 believers received an "infilling" with the Holy Spirit and testified to the wonders of God.

4. **Leading** – Luke 4:1

"Jesus…was led around by the Spirit in the wilderness…"

Jesus was directed by the Spirit to serve the purposes of God. In this situation, Jesus was tested. We too, should be open to the Spirit's leading, even if it involves trials and the testing of our faith. We want Him to be the One leading us daily.

5. **Empowerment** – Luke 4:14

"And Jesus returned to Galilee in the power of the Spirit…"

The Spirit's empowerment was evident in Jesus' ministry with those He encountered from place to place. There were many difficult situations that He faced, but He was empowered to be a witness of the Father's grace and truth.

We should not try to do life, ministry, or missions on our own. We need the Spirit's empowerment. This is what Jesus revealed to His followers just prior to His ascension (see Acts 1:8).

6. **Teaching** – Luke 4:15

"And He began teaching in their synagogues and was praised by all."

Jesus taught by word and by example. The Spirit worked in Him and through Him to teach truth to the world. We are to be Jesus' ambassadors in our world and also teach others through God's Word and personal example. This starts in our own home, neighborhood, workplace, church and community. It then goes out to the nations (see Matthew 28:19-20).

7. **Identification** – Luke 4:18

"THE SPIRIT OF THE LORD IS UPON ME, BECAUSE HE HAS ANOINTED ME..."

Jesus purposefully read Isaiah 61:1-2, a Messianic prophecy, and openly claimed His identity as the Messiah. He was not ashamed of Who He was.

As Christ-followers, the Spirit helps us to be bold in declaring what Jesus has done for us and who we've become by the grace of God. Our identity has changed and we are now children of God through Christ!

The Holy Spirit imparts God's anointing on each of us as Christ-followers. His continual convergence in our lives through various circumstances are to lead us in doing God's will.

We don't know how the Holy Spirit may want to use us, but we must be open and obedient. The following story is a challenge that I faced while in Thailand, which illustrates this.

Carry The Cross

The words came to me clearly, "Carry the cross!" This was the last night before our team was to depart and return to Chang Mai, Thailand.

I had been lying awake in the middle of the night, my mind reflecting on the events of the past week in this remote village. Then, the Holy Spirit spoke distinctly to me of my final assignment before leaving later that morning.

I got up and made my way to the primitive shelter that our YWAM Outreach team had used as a meeting hall at one end of the village. In the shelter, leaning against a wall, was a crude wooden cross. I had made this cross two days earlier out of scrap boards and then put it in the ground on the hill where a new school building was being constructed.

Earlier that evening I removed it and brought it to the shelter to use in a drama that our team performed for the villagers. It was a presentation of the Gospel about Jesus coming to die for the sins of all people. After the drama, the cross had been set aside as everyone went to stand outside around a fire and sing praises to Jesus.

Now, as I made my way down to the meeting hall, I realized that I was the only one awake at this early hour. The stars filled the clear sky and the glory of God's handiwork was evident all around me – it was different from anything I had experienced before.

Arriving at the shelter, I found the cross and put it over my shoulder. As I began walking up the dirt path to the top of the hill, I became overwhelmed with emotion and tears began to flow.

The Holy Spirit began speaking deep within my spirit, reminding me of the great price Jesus paid to redeem my soul for eternity. This was a sacred moment.

I had been called to "take up" the cross and follow what Jesus did thousands of years earlier. Each step up the hill, with Jesus looking upon me…brought a flood of emotion that I can't describe.

Upon reaching the top of the hill and putting the cross in place, I looked down upon the fourteen huts of the village, with the witchdoctor's hut at the farthest end. I realized in a powerful new way that Jesus cared about each person in this village in their primitive surroundings and native ways.

They lived as their ancestors did centuries ago, but now our team and others were bringing a new revelation of the living and true God to them.

All they had known before was the fear of evil spirits and the control of the village witchdoctor. They knew very well the power of the demonic realm, but had never known or realized the love and care of their Creator.

The Gospel message had again been delivered in word, deed, drama, and praises to God over the past week. Now, a rough wooden cross stood as a daily reminder for all to see that God had come to them, to buy them back from Satan who had enslaved them for generations.

The cross and its' message of Jesus Christ, the Son of God and Savior of all, would point them in the way of everlasting life.

It was a privilege to carry the cross that very special night. It brought me to a new "crossroads" in my spiritual walk with Jesus, a walk where the Holy Spirit would point the way and give the instructions. It was a unique convergence experience.

Jesus had told His disciples there would be more assignments after He left and returned to His Father. Just as He was "on assignment" to do His Father's business, so too, the Holy Spirit would lead them into new areas of ministry.

We are Jesus' disciples today, with a passion to "take up" our cross and follow Him through the ministry of the Holy Spirit and whatever the convergence experiences may entail.

Be listening…be obedient!

Revelation After the Resurrection

Prior to His death, Jesus very clearly revealed to His disciples Who the Holy Spirit is and what He will do. Jesus informs them of what is to happen in John 14:16-20, 26.

Jesus gives them additional revelation in John 15:26-16:15. Take some time to read these two key passages right now.

Write down the essential truths that Jesus reveals about the Holy Spirit.

This teaching about the Holy Spirit must have overwhelmed and possibly even confused the disciples. Jesus was talking about when He would leave them and they were not expecting that to happen.

It becomes evident that in the midst of the chaos of Jesus' arrest, trial, and crucifixion, the disciples forgot about this class – "Holy Spirit 101". They panicked instead.

But, after His resurrection and prior to His ascension, something life-changing happens. This is the turning point for Jesus' disciples and their future ministry. They experience the convergence dynamic imparted by Jesus. John 20:21-22 tells us:

"So Jesus said to them again, 'Peace be with you; as the Father has sent Me, I also send you.'

And when He had said this, He breathed on them and said to them, 'Receive the Holy Spirit'."

This is the first evidence of post-resurrection conversion.

These men had heard that Jesus was alive, but now they encountered Him personally. Did they still have some doubt? Possibly, but then something supernatural happens. Jesus breathes on them and imparts the Holy Spirit into them.

Jesus' Church was birthed when this occurred!

All of Christianity depends on the resurrection of Christ. The Apostle Paul, reveals in I Corinthians 15:17-19, that if Christ had not been raised, then we would all still be lost in our sin, without hope.

But, the resurrection opened the way of salvation to all who would believe and receive Jesus by faith through the Holy Spirit.

This is crucial to understand. The Church did not begin on Pentecost when the Holy Spirit came later in a unique manner. There were many who came to faith in Christ before He ascended and prior to Pentecost.

Paul speaks of Jesus appearing to a group of over five hundred "brethren" or believers at one time (see I Corinthians 15:6). Acts 1:15 (NIV) reveals that there were 120 "believers" gathered in a room prior to the special manifestation of the Holy Spirit on Pentecost. Pentecost was simply an expansion or additional in-gathering of Jesus' Church.

The Holy Spirit was very active 50 days before Pentecost in the lives of those who encountered Jesus alive. The Holy Spirit brings the rebirth in a person who accepts Jesus as the risen and living God.

It is clear from Scripture, that among the first born-again believers were ten of Jesus' original disciples (Judas Iscariot had taken his own life and Thomas was absent). He *"breathed on them"* to impart the Holy Spirit for salvation the day He arose.

The Promise of the Father

It gets even more exciting! Luke gives us the information on Jesus' final words regarding the Holy Spirit just prior to His ascension back to Heaven.

They are words of revelation and prophecy soon to unfold. They are words that would enlighten the disciples and other believers as to what was soon to happen to them. Let's examine two definitive Scriptures:

> *"And behold, I am sending forth the <u>promise</u> of My Father upon you; but you are to stay in the city until you are clothed with power from on high."* (Luke 24:49)

Jesus informs them that something of great significance is yet to happen. It would be a special work of the Father and the Son together. It was part of the plan to proclaim the kingdom of God on the earth.

This promise involved being clothed, baptized, or covered *"with power from on high"*. That was enough for the disciples to know. They needed to trust Jesus, obey Him, and wait until He sent the *"promise"* of the Father.

Let's continue into Acts for more revelation –

*"**Gathering them together, He commanded them not to leave Jerusalem, but to wait for what the Father had** promised, 'Which,' He said, 'you heard from Me; for John baptized with water, but you will be baptized** with **the Holy Spirit not many days from now.**"* (Acts 1:4-5)

God had more coming to them – a special gift.

It is worth noting that the NIV uses the phrase *"but wait for the* gift *my Father promised"* (Acts 1:4). This adds special insight into the nature of the blessing to come – it is a gift.

Jesus gives more detail and makes it clear what the *"promise of My Father"* is. It was a *"gift"* to be given to those who were already believers. This gift would be an immersion with the Holy Spirit in a divinely powerful way.

Being *"baptized* with *the Holy Spirit"* (Acts 1:5) involves an immersion or covering over, just like the water baptism of John the Baptizer, when he immersed repentant people in the Jordan River.

The water covered them over before they came up out of the water. So too, the Holy Spirit would completely cover or clothe believers with God's power from on high.

It is to our benefit that Jesus makes mention of John the Baptizer in this context. It helps us grasp what He was referring to regarding the *"promise of My Father"* that He sends.

Look at what John the Baptizer himself prophesied prior to Jesus coming to be baptized:

"As for me, I baptize you with water for repentance, but He who is coming after me is mightier than I...He will baptize you <u>with</u> the Holy Spirit and fire." (Matthew 3:11)

John was clearly referring to Jesus, as the Christ, and prophesied of what He would later do. He would *"baptize you <u>with</u> the Holy Spirit and fire"*. I believe the *"fire"* mentioned here is the zeal of the Holy Spirit in a believer.

I personally make the connection between this divine *"fire"* and what was prophesied in Isaiah 9:7, *"...The zeal of the LORD of hosts will accomplish this."*.

This is in regard to the ministry of the future Christ that would result in the increase of God's kingdom, which is the work of the Holy Spirit. God's zeal will be active throughout history.

I love it when Scripture connects the dots for us so we can see the complete picture of God's plan for His people.

It is obvious from what John the Baptizer states and what Jesus states, that the *"promise of My Father"* is being *"baptized with the Holy Spirit."*

Remember, Jesus was revealing that this gift from the Father would come after a person received salvation, as was demonstrated at Pentecost. In other words, there is something more that follows conversion to Christ. It is a unique filling with the Spirit, an additional convergence experience.

Jesus continues to inform the Apostles why is it so important that they wait in Jerusalem for the *"promise of My Father"*, before going out to witness about His resurrection. In Acts 1:8, Jesus says:

> *"but you will receive power when the Holy Spirit has come upon you; and you shall be My witness both in Jerusalem, and in all Judea and Samaria, and even to the remotest part of the earth."*

The Apostles were not to go in their own strength, but in the empowerment and anointing of the Spirit. Then the harvest of God would be brought in!

Did the disciples fully understand what was about to happen as they waited in Jerusalem? I doubt it. They just knew that Jesus gave the command and He would follow through with sending the gift of the Father in His time and His way.

The disciples were baptized *"in"* the Holy Spirit regarding conversion when Jesus breathed on them (John 20:22). They were baptized *"with"* the Holy Spirit, which was the gift or promise of the Father, on the day of Pentecost (Luke 24:49; Acts 1:5; 2:4).

The Father, Son, and Holy Spirit worked together in this manifestation of power on Pentecost. They have done and continue to do what will fulfill Their plan for bringing in the harvest of lost people, until Jesus returns in glory.

There are those in Christianity that have not fully examined or understood these words of Jesus and are fearful of being *"baptized <u>with</u> the Holy Spirit"*, as a result.

People tend to be afraid of what they don't understand. The disciples didn't understand this new phenomena Jesus was referring to, but when they experienced it, they operated in the power of it.

The Book of Acts reveals how the New Testament believers continued to experience the gift of the Father and the empowerment to live for and serve Jesus Christ.

The Holy Spirit was the means by which Jesus began building His Church and continues to do so. God does not always work in ways we expect. Therefore, it is important to have an open and teachable spirit, allowing Him to work His way.

What questions do you have about this revelation of Jesus to His followers? Have you been fearful of what you don't understand or haven't been accurately taught in the past?

It's good that you are reading and receiving insight now. Jesus calls us to accept what He sends – the *"promise of the Father"*, which is the gift of being baptized *"with"* the Holy Spirit after our being baptized *"in"* the Holy Spirit at our conversion.

Ask the Lord to help you embrace what He offers and be open to receive from Him all that He wants to impart.

Ask Your Heavenly Father

When Jesus was teaching His disciples about the importance of prayer, He gave specific instructions – see Luke 11:1-13.

He concludes this teaching by telling a story and then finishes it by saying:

> *"If you then, being evil, know how to give good gifts to your children, how much more will your heavenly Father give the Holy Spirit to those who ask Him?"* (Luke 11:13)

Jesus emphasizes to His followers that the work of the Holy Spirit is a "gift" to be asked for. We should be asking our heavenly Father to impart the power of the Spirit into our life through this wonderful "baptism".

The Apostles also refer to the *"baptism with the Holy Spirit"* as the *"gift of the Holy Spirit"* (Acts 10:45; 11:17).

What a blessing this is from our loving heavenly Father!

If you have not already received this *"gift"* or *"promise"* of the Father, are you open and willing to ask for it?

If you are a true believer in Christ, now is the perfect time to ask. Here is a suggested prayer:

"Heavenly Father, from my heart I ask you for the gift you that You promised through Jesus, Your Son. I desire to be baptized with the Holy Spirit now and receive all that You have for me as Your child. Father, I am yielded to You and Your will for my life. Come, Holy Spirit and baptize me with power from on high. In Jesus name I pray this. Amen."

Begin to praise God and declare Who He is, giving Him glory for His love, His grace, His goodness, and His mercy toward you. He loves you dearly!

The Rest is HIS-Story

As we read the epistles of the Apostle Paul and other New Testament writers we see evidence of the Holy Spirit's power and leading. We discover the amazing plan of God unfolding.

God is in control and we can be confident in what He is doing. I recognize that God had the first word in the beginning of world and He will have the last word at the end of the world. He is in charge.

Jim Cymbala, pastor of the Brooklyn Tabernacle, shares excellent insight on the Spirit's leading in his book, SPIRIT RISING: Tapping Into The Power Of The Holy Spirit. He points out:

"The Holy Spirit is God's only agent on earth. He was sent here to guide us. If you read the book of Acts, you'll see that a computer-mapping program didn't govern Paul's trips. The illumination of the Holy Spirit guided his path. In fact, the Spirit forbade Paul from going to some places – not because they didn't need to hear the gospel, but because God had another plan. And the apostle waited until the Spirit's direction could guide him into it." [1]

As you read "HIS-Story" in Scripture, may your faith increase to be more trusting of Jesus to use you through the leading of the Holy Spirit in the coming days.

Each time you read God's Word, the Holy Spirit will reveal more and more of His will in the eternal story He has ordained. It's an exciting discovery when you realize that you are a history-maker!

You are alive for such a time as this and can have a great impact in the lives of others for God's kingdom. God wants to use you.

Say this out loud – "God wants to use me!".

Put that statement on a note card and tape it to your bathroom mirror. For the next two weeks, say it every morning when you wake up...because it's true.

See what the Holy Spirit begins to reveal to you in those weeks. Keep a journal of what you are discovering because of your openness to Him.

Chapter 5 – Attributes of the Holy Spirit

Throughout the New Testament we discover numerous ways the Holy Spirit impacts people, both unbelievers and believers.

You'll be amazed at His incredible influence. He is at work in the following ways:

- He **testifies** of Jesus to the world.
  (John 15:26)

- He **convicts** the world concerning sin, righteousness, and judgment.
  (John 16:8)

- He **glorifies** Jesus.
  (John 16:14)

- He **enters** a believer's life at conversion.
  (John 3:5-8)

- He **dwells** in the believer.
  (Romans 8:11; Ephesians 2:22)

- He **affirms** believers as children of God.
  (Romans 8:14-16)

- He **teaches** believers about God's will.
  (John 14:26)

- He **helps** believers understand God's Word.
  (John 16:12-15)

- He **produces** spiritual fruit in believers.
  (Galatians 5:22-25)

- He **seals** those who belong to Christ.
  (Ephesians 1:13-14)

- He **edifies** believers through the process of sanctification to turn from sin.
  (Romans 8:5-11; Galatians 5:16-18)

- He **fills** believers.
  (Acts 4:31; Ephesians 5:18)

- He **empowers** believers in ministry and witnessing.
  (Acts 1:4-5, 8; Acts 4:31)

- He **guides** believers in ministry.
  (Acts 8:29, 39; 13:1-4; 16:6-7; 20:22-23)

- He **imparts** different kinds of spiritual gifts to believers.
  (Ephesians 4:11; Romans 12:6-8; I Corinthians 12:1-11)

- He **brings** forth prophesying and speaking in tongues through believers.
  (Acts 2:4; 10:44-47; 19:1-7)

- He **unites** believers into the one body of Christ.
  (I Corinthians 12:12-13)

- He **inspired** the writing of all Scripture.
  (II Timothy 3:16; II Peter 1:20-21)

- He **witnesses** to believers of God's covenant and forgiveness of sins ("testifies" NIV).
  (Hebrews 10:15-17)

- He **intercedes** for believers through a unique utterance or groanings.
  (Romans 8:26-27)

- He provides **access** to the Father.
  (Ephesians 2:22)

- He **speaks** Jesus' words and will to specific churches and to the Church today.
  (Revelation 2:7, 11, 17, 29; 3:6, 13, 22)

This list of numerous ways the Holy Spirit influences humanity should cause us to be in awe of His importance.

It appears to me that few churches today fully recognize this and fail to emphasize His work in reaching the unsaved, maturing the believer, building Christ's Church, and expanding God's kingdom.

Read this list over again and take time to look up the Scriptures that go with each of these actions.

Identify which of these works of the Spirit has impacted your life directly and highlight or circle them.

Different Ways He Works

Greg Laurie, a pastor and director of Harvest Ministries, points out the following insightful information regarding the work of the Spirit. He states:

"The Bible uses three different Greek prepositions in the New Testament to describe the different ways in which the Holy Spirit works in our lives. This verse (John 14:15-17) shows two of these ways, the third can be found elsewhere in Scripture (Luke 24:49).

1. He Works *with* Us as Nonbelievers (para).

Prior to our conversion to faith in Jesus Christ, the Holy Spirit convicts us of our sin and reveals Christ as the answer (see John 16:8). Some might dismiss His prodding as that of one's conscience. Yet it is the Holy Spirit who opens our eyes to our terminally sinful condition, exposing our need to turn our lives over to Jesus Christ.

2. He Comes *into* Our Lives When We Turn to Christ (en).

Once we accept Jesus Christ as Savior and invite Him into our lives, the Holy Spirit comes and sets up residence, so to speak. First, He starts the process of salvation in our heart. Jesus said, 'I assure you, no one can enter the Kingdom of God without being born of...the Spirit' (John 3:5). Second, He assures us that we have done the right thing. Scripture says, 'For His Spirit joins with our spirit to affirm that we are God's children' (Romans 8:16). Now He can begin changing us from the inside out and develop the new nature within us.

3. He Will Come *upon* Us to Empower Us as Believers (epi).

Jesus describes the dynamic empowering of the Holy Spirit upon our lives in Luke 24:49, where He said, 'And now I will send the Holy Spirit, just as my Father promised.' This is what the early Christians experienced in Acts chapter 2, and it dramatically emboldened their witness for Jesus Christ. This power is available to believers today. Scripture says of the giving of His Spirit, 'This promise is to you, and to your children, and even to the Gentiles – all who have been called by the Lord our God' (Acts 2:39)." [1]

Your Faith Story

What is your "Faith Story"?

- How did the Holy Spirit convict you of your sin?

- Who or what did He use to reveal your need for a Savior?

- Where or when did He reveal Jesus to you?

- How did you respond to His revelation?

If you've never done so, take a blank sheet of paper and write out your personal "Faith Story".

It is a testimony of what the Lord has done through the Holy Spirit to bring you to Himself. It is a story to be shared – God's story, because it is God's work in you!

Let me ask you directly, do you know right now that you have come into God's kingdom and are you one of God's children? If not, this may be your initial convergence experience. As Romans 8:16 states, *"The Spirit Himself testifies with our spirit that we are children of God."*.

The Holy Spirit is drawing you to put your faith in Jesus Christ and claim Him to be your Savior. Go ahead right now with a heart of faith – come to Jesus – just as you are.

Repent of your sins and believe that He died on the cross for you to forgive your sins. Tell Jesus that you believe He is God and are surrendering your life to Him right now. Thank Him for coming for you, loving you, dying for you, and rising from the grave for you.

Pray this in Jesus' name right now.

Now rejoice that you are His child and through the Holy Spirit begin living according to His Word, the Bible.

Call, text, email, or Facebook someone right now and tell them that you just accepted Jesus Christ as your Savior and Lord. Telling others is testifying to the eternal work the Holy Spirit has done.

The "Hope Line"

As the Director of the Seattle Urban Pipeline, a multi-faceted, inner-city ministry, I continually looked to the Holy Spirit's leading in reaching lost people for Jesus.

One specific aspect of ministry that He put on my heart was – **JESUS** billboards! I'll be honest, I tried numerous times to dismiss the leading of the Holy Spirit on this assignment. It seemed like it would demand too much of me and my ministry plate was already very full.

But, one day while in a prayer meeting with a number of ministry leaders, the Holy Spirit spoke to me through the prayer of another person. It came across as a word of the Lord just for me. It got my attention!

He revealed that I had an unfulfilled "assignment" and it was God's will that I not put it off any longer. I heard His voice very clearly and knew what I must do – organize the process of putting up billboards around the city of Seattle.

As I made this outreach opportunity known to others, the Lord provided people to sponsor the printing and installation of these billboards. There were 5 "**JESUS**" billboards put up on major highways. On a bright yellow background, the letters **J E S U S** where printed in bold red. Underneath was a toll-free phone number ending with the word -- **HOPE**! The "Hope Line" was established for call-in contact and prayer.

Another big part of the outreach was having volunteers take the calls of those who would respond to the billboards.

People accepted the challenge and when there were no volunteers available, the calls were transfered to my cell phone. What an experience it was! We answered the calls with the words – "This is the Hope Line. Jesus cares about you. How may I pray for you today?"

There is a vast harvest of souls in our world. Putting the name of **JESUS** before those of our society brought a variety of responses. I put them into five categories:

- **CURIOUS** – People that simply called to ask – "What is this about?" "Who's doing this?" "Why are you doing this?" People are very curious and this was an open opportunity to share Jesus' love and offer to pray for those callers.

- **CONFUSED** – People that were God-haters, evil-doers, and instruments of Satan, who tried to mock and intimidate us for doing this. They would curse God and those answering the call. I instructed the volunteers to simply say – "Jesus loves you and died for your sins.", then hang up and pray for them as the Holy Spirit led. These lost souls were in spiritual bondage and facing eternity separated from God.

- **COMMITED** -- People would call in and say, "Praise the Lord, I am so encouraged. I never thought I'd be driving to work each day and see the name of Jesus on a billboard. Thank you and keep it up!" Wow, how refreshing to get those calls and what a blessing to pray for other believers.

- **CONVICTED** -- People who came under the conviction of the Holy Spirit by simply seeing the name -- JESUS. Some had been raised in a church but went off into the world. Others had not heard the Gospel but their sin was destroying them and they needed hope and help. Others knew Christ, but had chosen to give in to sin and rebelled against Him. These people were desperate for God, and those who answered the call were able to point them to Jesus and pray with them for salvation or restoration.

- **CRISIS** – People who were abused, lonely, homeless, depressed, suicidal, and hurting. They needed prayer and encouragement. The Holy Spirit would give us a heart of compassion for these people and encouragement from the truth of God's Word. Praying with them gave them hope to not give up, but look to God in their crisis.

For those willing to get more help, we connected them with a local Christ-centered church in their community. As believers, we all serve the same Lord. We are not in competition, but in cooperation. The Holy Spirit used the Hope Line to bring a spiritual convergence to those receptive at a critical time.

Jesus made it clear why He came – *"For the Son of Man has come to seek and to save that which was lost"* (Luke 19:10). He has called us to take up His mission and reach out to those who need Him as their Savior. This is also the work of the Holy Spirit in our world today. He uses those who have been redeemed to also seek those who are lost.

What is the Holy Spirit leading you to do or get involved in to reach the lost of our world?

I appreciate so much the conviction of the Apostle Paul revealed in I Corinthians 9:22 – *"To the weak I became weak, that I might win the weak; I have become all things to all men, so that I may by all means save some."*

The Holy Spirit certainly used this "weak" man, when

I submitted to His leading. He can use you also, just ask Him. Keep asking Him.

Remember, Jesus does the saving of an individual, we have the privilege of being His workers in His harvest field (see Matthew 9:37-38). We get to share the Gospel – the good news of Jesus, the eternal hope of mankind.

Truck'n for JESUS!

The Holy Spirit can use anything to point people to Jesus. In 1981, while serving as pastor of a church in rural Michigan, I acquired an old, rusty, 1947 Dodge truck. It had sat for years beside an old barn near Battle Creek, Michigan. It appeared that the farmer had used it to haul rocks out of his field until it quit running.

For the next seven years, it was my "project". I realized that it would need to be dismantled piece by piece (often with a chisel and hammer) before I could begin restoring it.

One Monday, when I had my regular day off, I was working on a rusty fender, dreaming about when the truck would be put together, newly painted, and I'd be driving it through town. In the midst of my "day-dreaming", the Holy Spirit spoke to me – "Who's going to get the glory for this?". I heard Him again ask the question. I came under conviction, right there and then. That day, I made a covenant with Jesus, that when the truck was done, I would put on both doors a sign that said – **JESUS is LORD**.

The "Jesus Truck" has been driven down many roads and even freeways over the past 25 years. People notice... not just the restored old truck, but the name of the One who is to get all the glory!

Does seeing a sign on a vehicle saying, "**JESUS is LORD**" make a difference in the life of someone? I don't really know.

But, I do know when the Holy Spirit leads a person to do something like this, He can use it to point people to the Savior or encourage those who already know Him to be bold in sharing Jesus openly. Even if only one person comes to Christ through the sign, it will be wonderful!

I've noticed some people look away as I drive by, but there are others who give me a honk and "thumbs up" sign. I've had people roll down their window and say – "I agree with your sign". Others have thanked me for being bold.

I believe there are numerous "links" in the spiritual chain that leads people to Christ. This may be one simple link in exposing the truth about Jesus – He is LORD!

Offending the Holy Spirit

In the New Testament there are specific Scriptures that reveal some very critical issues dealing with offending and sinning against the Holy Spirit. Take some time to look at these Scriptures that reveal the following truths:

1. **LYING** to the Holy Spirit.
    (Acts 5:1-10)

2. **GRIEVING** the Holy Spirit.
   (Ephesians 4:30)

3. **QUENCHING** the Holy Spirit.
   (I Thessalonians 5:19)

4. **RESISTING** the Holy Spirit.
   (Acts 7:51)

5. **INSULTING** the Holy Spirit.
   (Hebrews 10:29)

6. **REJECTING** the Holy Spirit.
   (I Thessalonians 4:8)

7. **BLASPHEMING** the Holy Spirit.
   (Matthew 12:31-32)

These are each very serious matters and a believer must take warning not to offend the Holy Spirit at any time.

There are consequences that result if we intentionally choose to do any of these actions against the Holy Spirit.

According to Jesus, blasphemy against the Spirit will not be forgiven. From the context of the passage, the Jewish religious leaders had mocked or slandered the Holy Spirit by attributing His work to the Devil.

In doing so, they committed the "unpardonable sin". They also were rejecting Jesus as the Christ, who was operating by the Spirit in healing a demon-possessed man.

When a person rejects the Spirit's witness of Jesus in unbelief, that person will not be forgiven, but will face God's eternal judgment. The consequence is for eternity!

I know times in my own life when I have grieved the Holy Spirit because of my decision to sin. There have been other times when I have resisted Him and the way He was leading due to my own fears.

King David had to come to grips with his sin against God and resisting the Holy Spirit when he committed adultery and then tried to cover it up and go on as if everything were just fine.

In his prayer of repentance found in Psalm 51, he specifically pleads with the Lord:

"Do not cast me away from Your presence
And do not take Your Holy Spirit from me." (v. 11).

His heart was broken over his sin and his repentance was sincere. The same should be true of us.

Another time, David prays a heartfelt prayer, asking the Lord to reveal any sin that may be in his life that he is unaware of. In Psalm 139:23-24, he asks –

"Search me, O God, and know my heart;
Try me and know my anxious thoughts;
And see if there be any hurtful way in me,
And lead me in the everlasting way."

Other translations use the word "offensive" (NIV); "wicked" (NKJV); "grievous" (ESV) instead of "hurtful"(NASB). These all fit the description of personal wrongdoing and help us recognize our personal sin before God.

The Holy Spirit longs for every believer to pray this…often.

We don't always know what's in our heart, but the Holy Spirit can search our hearts and reveal any way we may have offended God in our thoughts, words, or actions.

We need His help to own up and admit our hidden sin by confessing to God. This is for our good and God's glory, even though often difficult. When we come clean with the Lord, He brings renewal and refreshing to our spirit.

Francis Chan, author of The Forgotten God, states, "Walking by the Spirit comes down to daily dependence on God. Sometimes the struggle with sin seems hopeless…but as you begin following the Spirit's leading more and more, you will see sin in your life less and less." [2]

This is the wonderful work of on-going sanctification through God's Spirit. He leads us into living a holy life for Christ.

Quenching the Spirit

Henry and Richard Blackaby, in Experiencing God Day by Day, share the following insight that admonishes believers to be obedient.

Quenching the Spirit

"Do not quench the Spirit."
I Thessalonians 5:19

"We cannot prevent God from accomplishing His work in the world around us, but we can quench His Spirit in our lives. God has given us the freedom to withstand the Holy Spirit's activity in our lives. When we ignore, disobey, or reject what the Spirit is telling us, we quench His activity in us.

The prophet Isaiah described the result: *'Hearing you will hear and not understand and seeing you will see and not perceive; For the hearts of this people have grown dull. Their ears are hard of hearing, and their eyes have closed, lest they should see with their eyes and hear with their ears, lest they should understand with their hearts and turn, so that I should heal them'* (Isa.6:9; Matt. 13:14-15). When you sin, the Holy Spirit will convict you of your need for repentance. If you habitually ignore Him and do not repent, your heart will grow hardened to God's Word.

If the Spirit speaks to you about God's will for you, and if you refuse to take action, a time will come when the Spirit's voice will be muted in your life. If you continually reject the Spirit's promptings, a day will come when you no longer hear a word from God. If you repeatedly stifle God's Word to you so that you are no longer sensitive to His voice, He will not give you a fresh word. Be wary of resisting the voice of the Spirit in your life. You may not always be comfortable with what the Spirit is saying to you, but His words will guide you to abundant life." [3]

I vividly recall a time in ministry when I was challenged and came close to quenching the Spirit. There was an instance when the Spirit spoke to me about having more compassion for the hurting people without hope who were living aimless, empty lives.

I asked how I was to become more compassionate and He revealed that I was to purchase a black clerical shirt and white collar so I would look like a priest. Then I was to walk the streets of Seattle offering to pray for people.

I had serious doubts about taking on this role and mission, realizing that I might find myself in some very uncomfortable situations. Besides, I thought this kind of ministry was for the more evangelist type.

God was calling me to a special assignment, but I was at the point of quenching the Spirit of God. He had a special plan and I was that special person to fulfill it.

Submission is always essential in not quenching the work of the Holy Spirit. I submitted and set out to fulfill my assignment.

I found a store selling clergy attire and purchased the black shirt and white collar. I decided on the day I was to go out and dressed the part.

The Spirit led me to begin by the Space Needle, downtown Seattle.

When the Spirit specifically revealed someone to me, I was to say – "I'm here praying for people today, may I pray for you?" Since I obviously looked like a clergyman, people recognized my profession as I approached them.

It was a challenging experience as I walked around the area by the Space Needle and then other parts of Seattle seeking to have the Holy Spirit point out certain people. He knew their hearts and what was going on in their lives.

As I approached some people, they would see me and then look away. But, when I came up and sincerely asked if I could pray for them, they surprisingly shared the struggle going on in their life, sometimes with tears.

These were divine encounters! I had no clue who I was going to meet or what they were going to say, but the Lord certainly opened my heart to have greater compassion for others through these contacts.

I continued going to the streets when the Holy Spirit prompted me and also felt led to give people a simple gift to further encourage them. I located a Christian resource company that would print quality cloth bookmarks. The bookmarks were white satin with the word HOPE in shiny red letters.

The Holy Spirit wanted people to have something tangible to remind them of God's love and promise, as well as the divine encounter that took place on the streets of Seattle.

People were so appreciative and seemed amazed that they were receiving this special gift.

I called them, "HOPE Ribbons" and they looked like this:

HOPE

*"For I know the plans that I have for you,
declares the Lord, plans… to give you a
hope and a future."*
**(Jeremiah 29:11 – The Bible)
There is HOPE for you…God does have
a plan for your life!
He cares and so do others…
Call the HOPE Line today.**

[1-800 - _ _ _ - _ _ _ _]

On one occasion, the Holy Spirit pointed out an elderly African-American woman standing along the waterfront of Seattle. She looked very frail. As I approached her and asked her if I could pray for her, she threw her arms around me and hugged me with all the strength she had.

She was weeping and cried out, "I love Jesus, but I'm a drug addict. I need God's forgiveness!"

She then let go of me and showed me the drug kit and needles hidden behind her socks. I was able to pray with her and give her a HOPE ribbon. She held it tightly and cried some more.

When I left her, I sensed that maybe her earthly life wouldn't last much longer, but that she did know Jesus loved and cared for her in spite of her struggles. I believe we will see each other again someday in Heaven, when we both are celebrating God's mercy, grace, and forgiveness in eternity.

I'm thankful for the command – ***"Do not quench the Spirit."***

Are you listening to the Holy Spirit's command? Let Him lead you and see what great things God will do.

Rejoice in God's Work in You!

Greg Laurie points out three more important works of the Spirit in the life of the believer. These are identified by the Apostle Paul, when he wrote to the Christ-followers in Ephesus. They are truths that are crucial for us to embrace.

Why God Gives Us the Holy Spirit (Ephesians 1:13-14)

"You might say that the Holy Spirit is our "identifying mark" as a Christian. In this text we see three specific reasons God gives us his Holy Spirit:

The Holy Spirit Is a Promise. Once again, Scripture reminds us that God has promised to send the Holy Spirit to all those who have heard the good news of the gospel and trusted Christ as Savior.

The Holy Spirit Is a Seal. The Holy Spirit serves as a mark of ownership, showing that we belong to God.

The Holy Spirit Is a Guarantee. The Holy Spirit also represents God's pledge to bring us to our final spiritual inheritance. This word could also be translated as a 'first installment' or 'deposit', signifying that his sealing in our lives is a foretaste of much more to come!

God gives us the Holy Spirit not only to enable us to live out the Christian life but to prove that we are precious in his sight." [4]

This revelation gives us great security. We can trust God to complete the miracle He has begun in us through the Holy Spirit.

When Satan tries to bring doubts and discouragement, by faith lay hold of what God has established for you. Then, persevere and stay on course.

Remember to always fix your *"eyes on Jesus the author and perfecter of faith."* (Hebrews 12:2). We have the victory in Jesus through the power of the Holy Spirit – celebrate it every day!

Chapter 6 – The Fruit of the Spirit

As we begin looking closely at the nine distinct characteristics or fruit of the Spirit, we recognize in each of them the attributes of Jesus.

We come to the realization that the Holy Spirit was sent to help us become more Christ-like. Our desire as His disciples is to imitate Him, as the Apostle Paul points out in Ephesians 5: 1 – *"...be imitators of God, as beloved children..."*. The Holy Spirit makes this possible in every believer.

The term "fruit" in the context of Galatians 5:22-23 can be understood as "virtues"; "character traits"; or "attributes".

The Spirit Filled Life Bible points out that "...the fruit of the Spirit is one unit and indivisible. When the Spirit truly controls the life of a believer, he or she produces all these graces." [1]

Prior to revealing the fruit of the Holy Spirit, the Apostle Paul calls believers to *"live by the Spirit"* (Galatians 5:16 NIV) and be *"led by the Spirit"* (Galatians 5:18 NIV).

This involves not giving in to the *"desires of the sinful nature"* (Galatians 5:16 NIV). We are constantly challenged by the temptations that surround us, as well as the struggles within us. The "vices" of the flesh are in contrast to the "virtues" of Christ, therefore we need the help of the Holy Spirit continually.

We are aware that we can have a beautiful vegetable garden planted and vegetables (fruit) growing, but if left unattended, the weeds sprout up and soon take over. Weeds need to be constantly pulled up and thrown out. The same is true of our fleshly or sinful desires.

The Life Application Bible notes, "The will of the Holy Spirit is in constant opposition to our sinful desires. The two are on opposite sides of the spiritual battle." [2]

This sounds like internal "civil war" to me. Even the Apostle Paul confessed to the internal struggle he faced (see Romans 7:15-24), so we are not alone in this challenge. The Holy Spirit dwells within every true believer and we can call upon Him to strengthen us in our continual battle against sin.

In commenting on Galatians 5:17, The Life Application Bible notes, "Paul describes the two forces at work within us – the Holy Spirit and our evil inclinations. Paul is not saying these forces are equal. The Holy Spirit is infinitely stronger, but we are weak. Left to our sin, we will make wrong choices. Our only way to freedom from our natural evil desires is through the empowering of the Holy Spirit (see Romans 8:9; Ephesians 4:23, 24; Colossians 3:3-8). [3]

The NIV Study Bible points out regarding the call to **"live by the Spirit"** (Galatians 5:16 NIV) that, "Living by the prompting and power of the Spirit is the key to conquering sinful desires." [4]

We can grow and mature in Christ-likeness as we yield to the Holy Spirit's leading day by day. This is the on-going sanctification process. Jesus wants to complete the good work that He has begun in us (see Philippians 1:6).

To *"live by"* and be *"led by"* the Spirit is dependent on *"abiding"* in Christ. Jesus tells us,

"Abide in Me, and I in you. As the branch cannot bear fruit of itself unless it abides in the vine, so neither can you unless you abide in Me." (John 15:4).

Anne Graham Lotz, daughter of Dr. Billy Graham, shares:

"To abide in Christ means to remain connected to Him so completely that the "sap" of His Spirit flows through every part of your being, including your mind, will, and emotions as well as your words and deeds. The "fruit" that you then bear is actually produced by His Spirit in you through no conscious effort of your own. If you and I want to be fruitful, we do not concentrate on fruit-bearing; we concentrate on our personal relationship with Jesus Christ." [5]

Sometimes we get confused about knowing if the Holy Spirit is truly leading us in a specific way or manner. The Life Application Bible points out:

> "If your desires would lead to the qualities listed in Galatians 5:22, then you know the Holy Spirit is leading you. At the same time, you must beware of confusing your feelings with the Spirit's leading. Thus, being led by the Holy Spirit involves the desire to hear, and the readiness to obey, and the sensitivity to discern between your feelings and his promptings." [6]

Let's identify, examine, and explore each of these spiritual virtues – the fruit of the Spirit. For each virtue I will provide the Greek word and definition from Strong's Exhaustive Concordance of The Bible and the filing number where it is located. This will provide accuracy to the interpretation of each virtue.

<u>LOVE</u>

The Greek word is "agape" (Strong's 26) meaning "love, affection".

The key is recognizing "Who" the Holy Spirit directs this love and affection toward in the believer's life.

We must go to Deuteronomy 6:4-9 for a fundamental understanding of what must occur in our lives. This specific command was given to God's people. There is a direct connection for Christ-followers regarding the fruit of love found in verse 5 – *"You shall love the Lord your God with all your heart and with all your soul and with all your might."*

The Holy Spirit directs our love toward the Lord God Almighty. This love is a devotion to God based on relationship.

"Agape" love is the greatest form of love. It is the love that Jesus showed when He gave Himself as a sacrifice for our sins. It is sacrificial in nature and essence.

Remember what Jesus said in response to the question, "Which is the greatest commandment?"

It is to *"Love the Lord your God with all your heart and with all your soul and with all your mind."* (Matthew 22:37 NIV). We are to be fully engaged in this.

The NIV Study Bible points out regarding the Greek word, "agapao", that it refers to "the commitment of devotion that is directed by the will and can be commanded as a duty." [7]

There are times in my marriage that I demonstrate my love out of duty to Vivian based on the vows and covenant I made to her at our wedding. My feelings of devotion aren't always what they should be, but I love her the same. Therefore as an act of my will, I keep my commitment and seek to be devoted to her.

Is our love (agape, agapao) from a heart of faith and devotion? Can it be demonstrated at times through willful duty? Again, this is all born out of a relationship with God. The Holy Spirit helps us to fulfill our devotion and duty.

If my love relationship with the Lord is right, it will carry over into my other relationships. Love will permeate those relationships as well. Jesus calls us to also love our neighbor as our self.

So, is it fair to say, that the way I love my neighbor reveals the way I love God? Certainly it is worth reflecting on. I am convinced that to know God is to love God! When we come to the realization of Who He is and what He has done for us, how can we not love Him?

Personal Reflection: Can you truly say from your heart that you love the Lord and would lay down your life sacrificially for Him, as He did for you? In what ways are devotion and duty to Jesus evident in your life?

<u>JOY</u>

The Greek word is "chara" (Strong's 5479) meaning "to rejoice, joy, gladness of heart" [from "chairo" (Strong's 5463) – "joy as a direct result of God's grace"].

It has been said that "mercy" is not receiving what we do deserve and "grace" is receiving what we do not deserve. As Christ-followers, we are eternally thankful for God's mercy and grace in our lives, right?

The "joy" virtue of the Holy Spirit deals with our response to God's grace in our life. How would you explain God's grace to you? Take some time to reflect on what you've received from the Lord that you do not deserve.

King David expresses his joy or gladness of heart for God's grace in many of the Psalms. Psalm 103 is a classic example, where he specifically identifies reasons for praising God and expressing joy. He proclaims in Psalm 103: 2-6 (NIV):

" Praise the Lord, O my soul, and forget not all his benefits – who forgives all your sins and heals all your diseases, who redeems your life from the pit and crowns you with love and compassion, who satisfies your desires with good things so that your youth is renewed like the eagles. The Lord works righteousness and justice for all the oppressed."

Look at the "benefits" of God's grace to us in Christ:

- Forgives all our sins.
- Heals all our diseases.
- Redeems our life from the pit.
- Crowns us with love and compassion.
- Satisfies our desires with good things.
- Renews us with strength like the eagles.
- Works righteousness and justice on our behalf.

These "benefits" are worth rejoicing over every day! Where would we be without these God-given benefits?

The Holy Spirit knows the importance of having us focus not only on Who God is, but also on what He has done on our behalf. When we come to grips with what we have received from Him, our expression will also be one of joy.

The Old Testament prophet, Nehemiah, proclaimed to the Israelites, *"...Do not be grieved, for the joy of the LORD is your strength."* (Nehemiah 8:10). This came after the prophet read the Book of the Law and the people wept as they listened to it.

Then, after Nehemiah encouraged them, the people began to *"celebrate with great joy, because they now understood the words that had been made known to them."* (Nehemiah 8:12 NIV).

The Holy Spirit points us to what is eternal and reveals the reason for true inner joy, not circumstantial happiness. The Apostle Peter, in writing to believers being persecuted for their faith, says:

> *"and though you have not seen Him, you love Him, and though you do not see Him now, but believe in Him, you greatly rejoice with joy inexpressible and full of glory,"* (I Peter 1:8).

Our faith relationship with Jesus brings forth this attribute by the Spirit – *"joy inexpressible"* – because we belong to Him.

How many of us aren't hindered from experiencing and expressing joy due to circumstances that have overwhelmed and discouraged us?

We each struggle with different matters in living from day to day, but the Holy Spirit desires to help us rise above them. By looking to Jesus and recognizing our source of eternal salvation, we choose to focus on the real reason for joy, rejoicing, and gladness of heart.

Listen to the Apostle Paul, who endured great hardship and persecution for Christ. He states:

> *"Therefore, since we have been justified through faith, we have peace with God through our Lord Jesus Christ, through whom we have gained access by faith into this grace in which we now stand. And we rejoice in the hope of the glory of God. Not only so, but we also rejoice in our sufferings…And hope does not disappoint us, because God has poured out his love into our hearts by the Holy Spirit, whom he has given us."* (Romans 5:1-5 NIV).

Grace, rejoicing, Holy Spirit…do you see the connection for the Christian?

This matter of having joy through the Holy Spirit is a continual challenge because we live in a fallen world. In the midst of an unstable and often chaotic world, filled with pressure and stress, the Apostle Paul gives us a command – *"Rejoice in the Lord, always; again I will say, rejoice!"* (Philippians 4:4).

The double emphasis in this verse comes because we are prone to <u>not</u> *"rejoice in the Lord"*. We often question why the Lord would allow certain things to come into our life or family. Satan will do whatever he can or use whomever he will to rob us of the joy we have in Jesus.

There are times that we have to choose joy and rejoicing as an act of our will. Lifting up the sacrifice of praise to God in the painful times of life will keep our focus on the truth and love of God, which never change.

In Luke 10:21 (NIV), we read – *"At this time Jesus, full of joy through the Holy Spirit, said, 'I praise you, Father, Lord of heaven and earth…"*. Jesus was rejoicing in the work of God being manifest in the disciples that He had sent out with His authority.

The Kingdom of God was advancing and it was exciting. The Holy Spirit was revealing the grace of God at work in changed lives and Jesus was *"full of joy"*.

One more comment on this. We, as believers are part of the kingdom of God. We must profess that truth continually. Scripture tells us, *"…for the kingdom of God is…righteousness and peace and joy in the Holy Spirit."* (Romans 14:17).

We are in Christ's kingdom – that's a fact that should bring great joy to our heart. We must look to the Holy Spirit to help us express joy in our daily living.

Personal Reflection: Is the joy of the Lord evident in your life? In what ways is it demonstrated? Do others recognize the joy of Jesus in you? When is it most difficult for you to choose joy?

PEACE

The Greek word is "eirene" (Strong's 1515) meaning "peace, rest – in contrast with strife; it denotes the absence or end of strife, a state of untroubled, undisturbed, well-being."

How do we come to exist in this state of peace? This sounds like utopia. What about the reality of living in a world torn apart by strife, selfishness, greed, and war?

God gives us the answer to having true peace. His Word encourages us to recognize the "key" to having internal, external, lasting peace. The following Scriptures point out what we must apply to experience this.

■ **Psalm 9:10**

*"And those who know Your name will put their **trust** in You,*
For You, O LORD, have not forsaken those who seek You."

■ **Psalm 56:3-4**

"When I am afraid,
*I will put my **trust** in You.*
In God, whose word I praise,
*In God I have put my **trust**; I shall not be afraid.*
What can mere man do to me?"

- **Psalm 91:2**

  "I will say to the LORD, 'My refuge and my fortress,
  *My God, in whom I **trust**!'"*

- **Proverbs 3:5**

  *"**Trust** in the LORD with all your heart,*
  And do not lean on your own understanding."

- **Isaiah 12:2**

  "Behold, God is my salvation,
  *I will **trust** and not be afraid;*
  For the LORD GOD, is my strength and song,
  And He has become my salvation."

- **Isaiah 26:3-4**

  "The steadfast of mind You will keep in perfect peace,
  *Because he **trusts** in You.*
  ***Trust** in the LORD forever,*
  For in GOD the LORD, we have an everlasting Rock."

■ **Isaiah 30:15**

> *"For thus the LORD GOD, the Holy One of Israel, has said,*
> *'In repentance and rest you will be saved,*
> *In quietness and **trust** is your strength…' "*

The "key" according to God regarding personal peace is trusting in Him. Who or what are we trusting in? It will determine whether or not we have peace in living out our life. Trust is the essential factor in our relationship with the Lord. It is a determining factor of whether we have His ***"rest"*** when others come against us or circumstances seek to undo us.

Read these Scriptures over again.

How is the Holy Spirit speaking to you directly right now through God's Word?

If you've lived for any length of time, you've experienced some level of fear. There have been times in each of our lives where we were not at peace or experiencing God's "rest" through the Holy Spirit.

I recall a year after serving with YWAM in Thailand and the Philippians that I was diagnosed with a tumor about the size of a grapefruit on my small intestine. I had been very healthy up to this point and had not experienced major surgery before.

I struggled with thoughts of, "Will it be cancerous?", "Will they have to remove a large part of my intestine?", "Will I have to eat differently after going through surgery?", "Will the tumor be attached to some vital organ?".

There was also the anticipation of being put under general anesthesia for the surgery and wondering if I will come out of it. A person starts to ask probing questions when a reality like this happens.

In the midst of the "waiting period" before having surgery, I asked the Lord to show me a Scripture to embrace during this time. The Holy Spirit put on my heart Psalm 119. There are 176 verses in this Psalm, a lot to hold on to.

But, as I began reading this Psalm, the Spirit revealed one phrase that is repeated often – *"preserve my life…"* (Psalm 119:25, 37, 40, 88, 107, 154, 159 NIV). As I highlighted that phrase over and over, I realized that I would only have peace by trusting the Lord to preserve my life.

He is the One who gives life and each moment of my life is in His hands.

As I began praying that phrase from Psalm 119, it brought me great confidence and rest. I trusted God to *"preserve my life"*.

He brought me through it, even amidst some complications after surgery. He is faithful and trustworthy.

The Apostle Paul may not have gone through any serious medical surgeries, but he faced numerous life-threatening circumstances. He encourages believers in Philippians 4:6-9 (NIV) with these words:

"Do not be anxious about anything, but in everything, by prayer and petition, with thanksgiving, present your requests to God. And the <u>peace of God</u>, which transcends all understanding, will guard your hearts and your minds in Christ Jesus. Finally, brothers, whatever is true, whatever is noble, whatever is right, whatever is pure, whatever is lovely, whatever is admirable – if anything is excellent or praiseworthy – think about such things. Whatever you learned or received or heard from me, or seen in me – put it into practice. And the <u>God of peace</u> will be with you."

There is no true peace apart from the *God of peace*, Who imparts the *peace of God* through the Holy Spirit to those who completely trust in Him.

Is there something you are anxious about right now? Is there a fear that keeps holding you back from experiencing God's peace and rest? The Apostle Peter encourages us to have peace by coming to Jesus and **"casting all your anxiety upon Him, because He cares for you."** (I Peter 5:7). He is a faithful Shepherd.

We must give over all the worries, cares, or anxieties we have to Jesus.

Tell Him right now what you're struggling with – He does care. Give them over, all of them. You might want to use this prayer:

"Lord Jesus, I give over to You the following persons or matters that have robbed me of having peace. They are _____.
I trust You with all my heart. I thank You that You are above each one. I ask the Holy Spirit to strengthen me now and guide me in the way of peace from this day forward. Amen."

A prayer to use daily in focusing your trust in God, was shared by a friend who was part of a group of pastors that I used to meet with on a regular basis. My friend has experienced peace in praying the following prayer at the beginning of each day. I'd encourage you to adopt it as your own daily prayer, it will strengthen you.

"Lord, today I choose to trust in Your sovereign control over all things. You have a plan and purpose for everything.

Lord, today I choose to trust in Your infinite wisdom. Your thoughts are not my thoughts, Your ways are higher than my ways.

Lord, today I choose to trust in Your unlimited power. Nothing is impossible for You.

Lord, today I choose to trust in Your perfect love which You displayed once and for all when You sent Jesus to die on the cross for me. Amen." [8]

116

Personal Reflection: Is Jesus your "Prince of Peace" (Isaiah 9:6)? In what area(s) do you have trouble looking to Him and trusting Him? Do you have the assurance that He is with you always as He promised (Matthew 28:20)? It is healthy to share with others in the body of Christ and allow them to pray with you and for you in your times of difficulty. The Holy Spirit wants to encourage you!

<u>PATIENCE</u>

The Greek word is "makrothumia" (Strong's 3115) meaning "patience, forbearance, long-suffering".

We often think of this attribute with regard to having patience or forbearance with people who are immature in their faith or do not act responsibly. But, this primarily refers to being patient *with* God and His work in our lives.

This is specifically identified in James 5:10-11,

> *"As an example brethren, of suffering and patience, take the prophets who spoke in the name of the Lord. We count those blessed who endured. You have heard of the endurance of Job and have seen the outcome of the Lord's dealings, that the Lord is full of compassion and is merciful."*

James points to Job as an example of showing patience, forbearance, and long-suffering with God in the midst of his suffering.

In the end, Job endured. He was vindicated and God was honored. The Lord chose to bring a double blessing into Job's life after his extreme trial ended.

None of us would want to go through the testing that Job did, but his life still testifies to us today.

James also makes reference to "the prophets" who persevered through difficult trials. Several that we would readily recognize in the Old Testament are:

Noah – His faith was tested and he suffered ridicule as he obeyed God and built the ark. He endured for 120 years in completing his assignment. We know the benefit of his perseverance.

Moses – His faith was tested through his 40 years in the wilderness after he fled Egypt, then dealing with the hard heart of Pharaoh and finally another 40 years leading the Israelites through the wilderness to the Promised Land. He was used mightily of God as he endured through each challenging situation.

Daniel – He was taken captive into Babylon as a youth even though he was a God-fearing person. He faced numerous tests of his faith, but endured and took a stand for the LORD. He was an example to his peers. Scripture records his testimony and it continues to speak into our lives about patience with God in fulfilling His plan.

Nehemiah – God called him to take on the huge task of rebuilding the walls of Jerusalem. He was threatened and faced opposition from others during this difficult assignment. The task was finished because he endured.

The writer of Hebrews reminds us of another individual who was patient with God:

"For when God made the promise to Abraham, since He could swear by no one greater, He swore by Himself, saying, 'I WILL SURELY BLESS YOU AND I WILL SURELY MULTIPLY YOU' And so having patiently waited, he obtained the promised." (Hebrews 6:13-15).

Abraham *"patiently waited"* twenty-five years before Isaac was born and this specific promise of an heir was fulfilled.

As we follow the Lord by faith throughout our life, there may be times when we are called upon to be patient with God and His sovereign ways.

It is natural for us to want to see God act now and in the way we expect, but He is the One Who is all-wise and as James told us – *"the Lord is full of compassion and is merciful"* (James 5:11). We must trust Him continually and walk in faith.

It should also be noted that James encouraged his readers with the following admonition:

"Therefore be patient, brethren, until the coming of the Lord. The farmer waits for the precious produce of the soil, being patient about it...You too be patient; strengthen your hearts, for the coming of the Lord is near." (James 5:7-8)

We are limited in our understanding and knowledge, but the Lord is unlimited. His ways are higher that our ways! He works according to His plan in our lives and calls us to be long-suffering in the process.

There was a time that the Lord called me to lead "Prayer-walks" through the streets of Seattle.

Then He expanded my assignment and I was to go up to the top of the Space Needle on a regular basis with Prayer Teams. We would pray over Seattle and the region from that high place.

On certain occasions, the Holy Spirit would lead me to take my shofar and blow it from the Space Needle to declare the authority and glory of the Lord.

At times our Prayer Team would gather and celebrate The Lord's Supper together from the Space Needle, as a testimony of the saving and sacrificial work of Jesus. It was a time of trusting God and believing He would work in His time and His way.

One evening as the Prayer Team was praying God's Word over the city, an intercessor on the team came up to me and shared – "Pete, the Lord has shown me that you are to be long-suffering with Him." I was a bit confused at first, but the more I reflected on what was spoken to me, I realized that the Holy Spirit wanted me to persevere in what He was calling me to do regardless of whether I saw the visible results or not.

Amidst all the "Prayer-walking" and other prayer assignments, no visible revival broke out in the city. But, God definitely was at work through our prayers. There was even a period of six weeks when there were no homicides in Seattle. This made headlines in the Seattle Times since it was so rare. We know there is a powerful impact in the spirit realm when we pray as led by the Holy Spirit.

That intercessor's input gave me insight that kept me moving forward in obedience to fulfill God's will – whatever it may be.

I believe as we are patient with the Lord and allow the Holy Spirit to use us in whatever context it may be, that He accomplishes His plan through us.

We also have the example of the Apostle Paul. He relates his personal challenges in ministry for Jesus and the kingdom of God,

> *"but in everything commending ourselves as servants of God, in much endurance, in afflictions, in hardships, in distresses, in beatings, in tumults, in labors, in sleeplessness, in hunger,"* (II Corinthians 6:4-5)

Do you struggle with God's timing and ways? Do you sometimes wonder – "What's the use in continuing, I'm not seeing any results to my obedience?" Let me encourage you to seek the help of the Holy Spirit regarding this attribute of patience.

King David expresses his challenge in being patient with God. He states in Psalm 27:13-14:

"I would have despaired unless I had believed
that I would see the goodness of the LORD
In the land of the living.
Wait for the LORD;
Be strong and let your heart take courage;
Yes, wait for the LORD."

We wait *for* the Lord by being patient and long-suffering *with* the Lord through life. I personally believe that, in Heaven, the Lord will reveal to us how our patience and endurance in ministry and missions was used to impact lives for eternity.

Personal Reflection: What test of endurance are you facing right now in your life? How is God calling you to wait on Him? Have you struggled with enduring through hardship in the past, wondering if God is really at work? Let the example of others in Scripture strengthen and give you hope as you seek to do God's will. Take the opportunity to share your challenge with others who can support and pray with you through this time.

KINDNESS

The Greek word is "chrestotes" (Strong's 5544) meaning "kindness, gentleness, graciousness".

The Complete Word Study of the NT states that it, "Denotes that apparent and ready good will, usually manifested in friendly, considerate demeanor, and especially in the practice of hospitality, readiness to help, tenderness, cherishing and maintaining fellowship." [9]

The key concept of this attribute or work of the Holy Spirit in the believer is that of having a gracious manner of dealing with others.

Several examples (and there are many) from the ministry of Jesus reveal how He applied kindness. They are as follows:

■ **Matthew 8:1-4** – A man with leprosy came to Jesus and asked to be healed. Scripture tells us – *"Jesus stretched out His hand and touched him, saying 'I am willing; be cleansed.' And immediately his leprosy was cleansed."(v. 3)*

It was against the Jewish rules to touch a leper! Jesus chose to show extreme kindness by being personal, even if it meant breaking the religious and cultural rules, to impact the suffering man.

How often are we willing to go beyond what's expected to sincerely impact another person's life with an act of kindness? Jesus didn't care about His reputation; He cared about the person in need.

■ **Matthew 8:5-13** -- Next, we find that a Roman centurion comes to Jesus on behalf of his sick servant. Jesus dialogued with the Gentile man and saw in him a unique level of faith in God. He complimented the man for his great faith and granted his request without even going to his house.

Jesus didn't show partiality by only caring about those of His own nationality, the Jews, but also extended God's kindness to the Gentiles.

Have we set boundaries on who we will help and reach out to? Have we decided who is deserving of our acts of kindness and who is not?

■ **Matthew 8:16, 28-34** – Jesus even showed kindness to those who were demon-possessed. This is where things can get uncomfortable. Isn't it best to avoid these people? Jesus didn't. He showed kindness to those in bondage to Satan and his demons. He delivered them and restored them. God's kindness knows no limits! This is a constant challenge to us because there are those all around us that are hard to love.

It's been said that, "Hurt people, hurt other people". From my experience in Christian ministry over the years, I would have to agree. A person's behavior often reveals what is going on inside them. We need to look beyond what's happening on the outside and seek to show the kindness of God to impact a person's heart.

■ **Matthew 9:36** – Jesus didn't just see people massed together in a multitude, He saw into their individual hearts and lives. Jesus saw individuals in the crowds who needed God's kindness, grace, and love. This Scripture tells us, *"Seeing the people, He felt compassion for them, because they were distressed and dispirited like sheep without a shepherd."*

The NIV states that the people were *"harassed and helpless"*. Jesus knew how Satan had deceived these people. He knew how confused these people were. He knew they were merely existing – living without hope.

Compassion is kindness in action – it gets involved to make a difference regardless of the sacrifice involved. Jesus *"felt compassion"* and demonstrated it throughout His ministry. He was moved in His spirit over the condition of those around Him.

He knew He would be making the "ultimate sacrifice" as the true Shepherd for lost, hurting, and hopeless people. He knew this degree of kindness would change people through the ages who would accept Him and receive this great work of God by faith for spiritual healing.

There are many "distressed and dispirited" people all around us. It may be that they are struggling with depression, bi-polar syndrome, panic attacks, shame, guilt, fear, or some other condition. Often these people are very unstable and unpredictable.

We need the help of the Holy Spirit to give us discernment regarding how to reach out and help those struggling with these and other difficult mental, emotional, and spiritual conditions.

■ **II Corinthians 6:3-6** -- The Apostle Paul lists the many hardships that he endured in ministry. Through them all, he chose to act right when others were treating him wrong. He points out in verse 6 – *"in purity, in knowledge, in patience, <u>in kindness, in the Holy Spirit</u>, in genuine love,"* Paul needed the Holy Spirit's help to show kindness and so do we, everyday. He wants us to ask Him continually to do what's right when others treat us wrong.

In ministry and missions the saying is very true – "People don't care how much you know, until they know how much you care."

Every church should have the compassion of Jesus evident in how they do ministry. This means the church should be outward focused, seeking to reach out to those in the community with extra challenges. Providing a safe place to come, share, and be accepted.

Celebrate Recovery, is a program started by Saddleback Community Church in southern California. It is designed to help those with various addictions and has been very effective in providing a caring atmosphere of acceptance. Thousands are involved in many churches across the United States and are finding help and hope.

Kindness through the Holy Spirit also has to do with one's personal demeanor. Our demeanor is our attitude expressed in our actions or behavior. It involves how we relate to others.

Do we display a "grace-filled" or gracious attitude toward others? Or, do we tend to find fault, criticize, and point out the flaws in others?

Of course, we want God's grace for our own lives and we want others to be gracious to us – but, are we doing the same in our relationships? How would others truthfully assess your demeanor?

Yielding to the Holy Spirit will make all the difference in the world as to how we relate to others.

Personal Reflection: Do you see yourself as being a compassionate person? Does your heart feel the pain that others may be going through? Are you willing to make sacrifices to help others in distress and facing difficult situations? Kindness is a key action in modeling Christ to others. This may not be your natural temperament, but it is to be the fruit of the Spirit evidenced in you. Ask Jesus to show you the wonders of His grace toward you. Then seek out someone you can be gracious and kind to. This is not "paying it forward", this is "paying it upward" to bring God glory.

<u>GOODNESS</u>

The Greek word is "agathosune" (Strong's 19) meaning, "goodness".

The Complete Word Study of the NT states, "It is character energized expressing itself in active good...A

127

person may display his zeal for goodness and truth in rebuking, correcting, chastising." [10]

An example of this would be when Jesus demonstrated righteous indignation in cleansing the Temple (Matthew 21:12-13).

The Holy Spirit desires to help us respond to people and situations, not react to them. Jesus responded to the situation at the Temple because of His love for the Father and zeal to reveal true righteousness in the place of prayer. He was in control in His display of "goodness".

When there is a need to address an issue or correct a problem, as Christ-followers we are to check our own heart first. Jesus pointed out the importance of removing the log in our own eye, before pointing out the speck in someone else's.

We know this, but have a hard time applying this when our emotions are running high. *How* we say or communicate something is just as important as *what* we say or communicate! We may say the right thing in the wrong way and it creates a bigger problem. Relationships take work with the help and leading of the Holy Spirit.

Goodness doesn't ignore a problem, but deals with it in the right way and for the right reason. This trait of the Holy Spirit denotes seeking to overcome evil with good. It seeks to rightly correct the wrong that is taking place.

When my wife and I were team leaders in Thailand and the Philippines with YWAM in 2001, we sensed the Holy Spirit leading us to choose a "Team Scripture". In praying about this, the Holy Spirit brought Colossians 3:12-

14 to us and we presented it to the team. They embraced these verses and we read them aloud often.

We knew that in the midst of our mission outreach, with uncomfortable and challenging circumstances, there would most likely be conflicts between team members. Those who have been on either short-term or long-term missions know this often does happen. Issues need to be addressed in a manner of goodness.

In order to display a zeal for goodness in whatever situation might arise, we wanted God's Spirit and God's Word to guide us in the process. Look closely at what this passage reveals about how believers are to interact with each other:

> *"So, as those who have been chosen by God, holy and beloved, put on a heart of compassion, kindness, humility, gentleness and patience; bearing with one another and forgiving each other, whoever has a complaint against anyone; just as the Lord forgave you, so also should you. Beyond all these things put on love, which is the perfect bond of unity."* (Colossians 3:12-14)

Our team was tested on this! Not just once, but several times in different situations. As team leaders, Vivian and I applied the attribute of goodness in these situations, addressing the matters and allowing the Holy Spirit to bring resolution. It is not pleasant to confront negative issues, attitudes, or behavior, but it is necessary for the good of everyone and to have effective ministry.

This virtue is to be evident and applied in the body of Christ continually. If church leaders would demonstrate goodness among each other and call the fellowship of believers they are leading to do the same, what a difference it would make. There may be less people who leave a church over hurt and unresolved issues. There may be less church "splits". There may be more pastors who stay longer to serve at a church. This is an area that needs serious attention. The Apostle Paul points out:

"for you were formerly darkness, but now you are Light in the Lord; walk as children of Light (for the fruit of the Light consists in all goodness and righteousness and truth), trying to learn what is pleasing to the Lord." (Ephesians 5:8-10)

It truly does please the Lord when we are bright lights for Him and display the godly attribute of goodness in our daily living. The *"fruit of the Light"* comes forth from the believer by the Holy Spirit's power.

It's good to do some regular self-examination. How would you honestly assess your level of spiritual illumination shining into the lives of others?

Paul commends the believers in Rome saying:

"And concerning you, my brethren, I myself also am convinced that you yourselves are full of

goodness, filled with all knowledge, and able al-
so to admonish one another." (Romans 15:14)

What an honor to be commended for being *"full of goodness"* and able to *"admonish one another"*. Admonishing involves rebuking and not everyone apprec-iates or is willing to be rebuked. It is part of our maturing process, though.

The Apostle Paul needed to admonish or rebuke the Apostle Peter because he was not honoring the Gentile believers as he should (see Galatians 2:11-14). I'm sure this was an uncomfortable encounter, but necessary. It set Peter straight in the matter of Jew-Gentile relationships as Christ-followers.

Some people mean well, but come off intense or harsh to others. There are the "truth-tellers", who tell it bluntly like it appears to them, regardless of who they alienate. Then, there are the "grace-givers", who are too cautious and avoid conflict because they want to keep the peace at all cost. Both are in error.

The fruit of goodness is characterized most clearly in Jesus. The Apostle John reveals that He was *"full of grace and truth"* (John 1:14). John continues to enlighten us by saying:

> *"For of His fullness we have all received, and grace upon grace. For the Law was given through Moses; grace and truth were realized through Jesus Christ."* (John 1:16-17)

People caught up in legalism or a "religious spirit" are out of the will of God. They are not accurately following Jesus' example. We should exemplify Him by being "graciously truthful" in our interactions, showing goodness immersed with grace. We must continually recognize the fullness of God's grace toward us.

My experiences in Christian ministry have taught me a lot about people. They have also taught me a lot about myself. I've learned that the way I treat people reveals what's going on inside of me. I don't always like what I see. Praise God, the Holy Spirit is willing to bring me in line with Jesus if I am willing to let Him.

What's the bottom-line on this attribute of goodness? I believe that through the Holy Spirit, it allows us to be part of the solution, not add to the problem.

Personal Reflection: Do you lean toward being a "truth-teller" or a "grace-giver"? Have you asked the Holy Spirit to line you up with Jesus and His character? Do you tend to be a "peace-keeper" avoiding conflict and not resolving differences? Have you asked the Holy Spirit to help you change to be a "peace-maker", even though it may be hard? Are you part of a leadership team or serving in some capacity of leadership? If so, be willing to admonish others in appropriate ways when necessary, it will help build and strengthen the team.

FAITHFULNESS

The Greek word, "pistis" (Strong's 4102) means "faith, being persuaded, belief, fidelity, faithfulness".

This attribute denotes a firm persuasion or conviction. It specifically refers to faith in God.

What Biblical characters come to your mind when you think of examples of faithful people?

We have examples from Genesis to Revelation of those who had a faith relationship with the living God and were faithful in living it out. But, a special list of individuals is recorded in Hebrews 11. This one chapter names those we can look to as examples of faithfulness. We often refer to them as "hero's of the faith".

First, note these two crucial matters:

- ■ Hebrews 1:1 reveals that true faith involves belief and being persuaded so that action results.

- ■ Hebrews 1:6 reveals the importance of believing God initially and then diligently continuing in that belief.

Numerous individuals are identified in Hebrews 11 as living faithful lives. Their character is highlighted by that of faithfulness to God.

Turn in your Bible to Hebrews 11 for a moment and read through the verses. Let God's Word encourage and inspire you.

I believe that out of personal conviction of truth comes a walk of obedience to God. In reality, we live what we believe.

Did you notice in reading this passage that the writer inserts a special section at the end? The majority of verses point out what we would call "victories" as a result of living in faith. But, verses 35b-39a reveal another side to faithfulness – persecution and martyrdom.

Look again at God's perspective shown here:

"...and others were tortured, not accepting their release, so that they might obtain a better resurrection; and others experienced mocking and scourging, yes, also chains and imprisonment. They were stoned, they were sawn in two, they were put to death with the sword; they went about in sheepskins, in goatskins, being destitute, afflicted, ill-treated (men of whom the world was not worthy), wandering in deserts and mountains and caves and holes in the ground. And all of these, having gained approval through their faith..." (Hebrews 11:35b-39a)

There is the high cost of being a faithful disciple of Jesus – your very life! This shouldn't surprise us. Remember what Jesus said was the requirement for being His disciple? Let's allow Him to tell us:

"Then Jesus said to his disciples, 'If anyone wishes to come after Me, he must deny himself, and take up his cross and follow Me. For whoever wishes to save his life will lose it; but whoever loses his life for My sake will find it."
(Matthew 16:24-25)

Jesus was very clear. In actuality, He was saying – "If you're not willing to die for Me, don't even consider following Me!"

There is a reason that Jesus mentions the "cross" here, long before He would place Himself on the cross of Calvary. He was seeking followers who would be fully devoted to Him, no matter what the cost to them.

Jesus seeks those who will be faithful to Him to the end, no matter what they will have to experience in the journey.

Our world has been shocked by the brutal murders of Christians in Egypt and other parts of the Middle East by ISIS and various radical Muslim groups. It is an atrocity! Those who stood firm in their faith in Jesus have served as a testimony of what it truly means to be a Christ-follower.

We know Christian martyrdom has taken place continuously since the death of Steven, the first one to die for his faith in Jesus (see Acts 7:60). We also must be ready and willing, as we see an increase in persecution happening today.

Back to Hebrews 11 – it appears in this chapter on faith and the way of faithfulness, that some were delivered and others defeated. Not so! Verse 39 reveals the eternal perspective, which is what really counts – *"And all of these, having gained approval through their faith..."*. God's approval is the approval we should desire. Faith in Him and faithfulness to Him indicate approval according to this passage of Scripture.

When it's all said and done, will you be approved by God for your faith demonstrated by your faithfulness?

As Jesus revealed in the parable of the talents in Matthew 25:14-30, the master (God) desires to say – *"Well done, good and faithful servant, you were faithful..."* (v. 21 NKJV). Will you hear these words one day when you give an account to the Lord?

The Apostle Paul helps us understand more about this attribute of the Holy Spirit when he states:

"I have fought the good fight, I have finished the course, I have kept the faith; in the future there is laid up for me the crown of righteousness..."
(II Timothy 4:7-8a)

We are each called to finish well! The Holy Spirit will enable us if we seek His help in whatever test, trial, or hardship we may face before we graduate into Glory and receive *"the crown of righteousness"*.

The Bible reveals the good, the bad, and the ugly of humanity. There are those who started well with God, but became unfaithful. They are a negative example of what can happen to a person who proves to be unfaithful. In the

Old Testament, we can look at Cain, the first child of Adam and Eve; King Saul, the first king of Israel; and even Solomon, who was given wisdom from God but chose to be influenced by his many foreign wives and their pagan beliefs.

We can also point to some in the New Testament such as, Ananias and Sapphira (Acts 5:1-10), Phygelus and Hermogenes (II Timothy 1:15), Demas (II Timothy 4:10) and others. Unfaithfulness to the Lord was evident in each person, which brought about serious consequences.

We must take seriously the warning throughout Scripture, especially in Hebrews 6:4-6:

"For in the case of those who have once been enlightened and have tasted the heavenly gift and have been made partakers of the Holy Spirit, and have tasted the good word of God and the powers of the age to come, and then have fallen away, it is impossible to renew them again to repentance, since they again crucify to themselves the Son of God and put Him to open shame."

This warning should result in each of us having a respectful "fear of the Lord" (see Hebrews 3:5-14), so that we do not neglect to walk in faith and obedience before Him.

Christ gave His all for us; we are to give our all for Him.

Personal Reflection: Are you a true disciple of Jesus? How is this evident in your life?   How much are you willing to suffer for Christ?   How is He calling you to be faithful right now?   Is there a faith assignment He has called you to fulfill?   Seek the help of the Holy Spirit to "finish" well.

GENTLENESS

The Greek word is "praotes" (Strong's 4236) and means "gentleness, humility, meekness".

This attribute denotes true meekness or humility before God and then before others. It is a virtue born in strength of character that is under submission to authority.

An excellent illustration of meekness is that of a wild stallion that is tamed and now submitted to its master. The animal still has incredible strength, but it has submitted by an act of its will to the one who has tamed it or is riding it.

The attribute of gentleness is the same with a person's will being submitted to God and His control.

There is an Old Testament individual who is identified with this outstanding characteristic. Scripture points out this person in Numbers 12:3 –

"Now the man Moses was very __humble__, more than any man who was on the face of the earth."

The King James Version states,

"Now the man Moses was very <u>meek</u>, above all the men which were upon the face of the earth.".

Moses was a pillar of strength, once the prince of Egypt and possibly in charge of Pharaoh's army. But, after becoming a fugitive for killing an Egyptian taskmaster and spending forty years as a shepherd in the desert, he was "tamed".

This strong-willed, powerful man now submitted himself to the highest authority – Almighty God. He became God's servant and displayed the character of gentleness in delivering the people from Egypt and leading them to the Promised Land.

He was God's man, but only because he was humble before God first, as well as, humble before the people of Israel as their leader.

Note what Jesus says about the attribute of meekness in the Beatitudes – *"Blessed are the gentle, for they will inherit the earth."* (Matthew 5:5). The NIV, ESV and NKJV translates this – *"Blessed are the meek…"*.

The condition of being *"Blessed"* has great significance for those in Christ. It denotes "God's favor". This is the place where we all should want to be, right? Those who are meek or gentle in character will *"inherit the earth"*.

I take this to mean that the Holy Spirit will use the meek or humble person to impact people and situations on earth for God's kingdom. They will be "world-changers" by God's power. This attribute is a qualifier for those who are going to have a spiritual influence for Jesus in the lives of others.

Have you found it to be true that pride is repulsive and repels people? True humility attracts people.

It must be known that meekness is not weakness. Just the opposite! The meekness or gentleness of a person controlled by the Holy Spirit brings admiration and respect.

There is another example given for us in Scripture. The supreme example of meekness is in Jesus, the Son of God. In Matthew 11:29, Jesus testifies about Himself and His Godly character, saying:

"Take My yoke upon you and learn from Me, for I am gentle and humble in heart; and YOU WILL FIND REST FOR YOUR SOULS."

The One who has all authority in Heaven and on earth reveals that He is *"gentle and humble"*. This is meekness at its best.

The Apostle Paul was inspired by the Holy Spirit to give us revelation into the meekness of Jesus. He reveals:

"Have this attitude in yourselves which was also in Christ Jesus, who, although He existed in the form of God, did not regard equality with God a thing to be grasped, but emptied Himself, taking the form of a bond-servant, being made in the

likeness of men. Being found in appearance as a
man, He humbled himself by becoming obedient
to the point of death, even death on a cross."
(Philippians 2:5-8)

Jesus, as God and the Son of God, did what no one else could ever do – humbled Himself to become the God-man. He entered into humanity by submitting Himself to the Father's will, lived among humanity in the flesh, and then died on the cursed cross for lost mankind.

Jesus had the power to call forth 12 legions of angels (Matthew 26:53) – that's 72,000 angels! They would have destroyed the world. All He had to do was give one simple command – one word. The angels were ready to act. Talk about power under control, there you have it. The One who said *"I am gentle and humble in heart"*, demonstrates what the virtue of gentleness is all about.

This character of Christ should be demonstrated among pastors, missionaries, leadership in churches, and leaders of national ministries. Too often, there is conflict and fallout because certain people want to control the ministry or operation of it. Humility goes out the window when other "agendas" come into play. Leaders are out of character with Christ when they want their way. They ignore the One who set the standard as their model of serving in ministry.

Regretfully, after serving in pastoral and para-church ministry, I have encountered those who where Christ-followers, but unwilling to be gentle, humble, or meek in the leadership part they played. Sometimes their actions proved to be self-serving instead of God-serving, but they couldn't see it. Respect, love, and caring for fellow-leaders were replaced by anger, mistrust, and accusation.

This must grieve the heart of God! It certainly doesn't bring Him glory and often results in a division between those who are supposed to be on the same team. The Holy Spirit's work is not evident when man's will and ways take priority.

I have sought in every church and ministry the Lord has called me to, to have the goal of making Jesus known and helping others to follow Him. Have I messed up at times? Certainly. Under the conviction of the Holy Spirit, I have asked for forgiveness to those involved, sometimes with tears. It is hard, but right. We learn the lessons of humility and meekness when we fail, then obey.

It is true, that the way up is by bending down. God always honors humility and helps us grow spiritually.

We should not overlook a life-lesson in humility that I'm sure the first disciples never forgot. It took place on the night Jesus was betrayed by Judas, as they partook of the Passover Meal. Look at what took occurred:

"Jesus, knowing that the Father had given all things into His hands, and that he had come forth from God and was going back to God; got up from supper, and laid aside His garments; and taking a towel, He girded Himself. Then He poured water into the basin, and began to wash

the disciples' feet and to wipe them with the towel with which He was girded." (John 13:3-5)

Jesus is the Master. He did what each of the disciples refused to do. It was the servant's job to wash the feet of those present in the room. Jesus showed them first-hand what it means to be submitted to God and others. He used this situation as a "teaching moment" to leave an impact on each of them regarding what God looks for.

Jesus explained His action of servant-hood, to make sure His disciples would really get it. John 13:14-17 tells us what Jesus said:

"If I then, the Lord and the Teacher, washed your feet, you also ought to wash one another's feet. For I gave you an example that you also should do as I have done to you. Truly, truly, I say to you, a slave is not greater than his master, nor is one who is sent greater than the one who sent him. If you know these things, you are blessed if you do them."

Note that Jesus instructs His followers saying *"you also ought to"* serve one another in a humble manner. We are blessed and will have God's favor "if" we do what we "ought to". The choice is always ours in serving others. Are we truly willing to submit to the Holy Spirit and allow Him to use us to serve others through the attribute of gentleness? It's our call.

When serving with YWAM in the Philippines, our team lived in an old house at the mouth of Manila Bay. It was part of a small village where most of the men fished for a living. As we moved into the house on the waterfront, I noticed the fishermen standing by their boats just beyond our residence. I waved to them and they just stared back.

That evening, our team gathered together to worship the Lord and also pray for guidance as to how to reach the villagers with the love of Jesus.

The next morning there were children and youth in our front yard, waiting to meet all the new foreigners. They were curious, as well as hopeful that we had gifts to give them as others may have done in the past.

My attention was drawn to the fishermen and their boats. They had just returned from setting their nets at 3 a.m. and then pulling them up to check them at 7 a.m. I went down to watch them mending their nets. They did not speak English, so I couldn't understand what they were saying.

Then, I noticed something – many of the boats were painted on one side, but not the other. This seemed strange to me. Later that day, I asked a villager who knew some English why this was. He explained that the fishermen didn't have enough money to buy paint to finish their boats. It was a struggle just to keep their family fed on the few fish they caught each day.

As a pastor, I had come prepared to preach to these people, whether by myself or through an interpreter. But, as I was informed of the situation with the unfinished boats, I heard the Holy Spirit say – "Don't preach, just paint!"

God wanted me to be a servant to these villagers, old and young alike. Yes, our team was to interact with the children and youth, many of whom could speak English, but also seek to connect with the older adults who needed to know the love of Christ.

The next day, I made my way into the small town to find a hardware store. I had noticed the colors of some of the unfinished boats – red, blue and green. I decided to start with painting the red boat and purchased two quart cans and a brush. When I returned, I went up to the man with the unfinished red boat and motioned for him to open the can.

He thought I was trying to give him the paint, for him to do the work. When I wouldn't give it to him, but tried to pry off the lid with a stick, he got the idea and took out a jackknife with an opener on it. He opened the can and I began painting his boat. There was a shocked look on his face and then he started shouting to his fellow-fishermen something about an "Americano". He was pointing at me and all the others came over and were watching me. I finished his boat that afternoon.

That evening I shared with our team what transpired. They had been doing activities involving the children and youth most of the day. We continued to pray for the Holy Spirit to lead us in this month of outreach.

The next day, I sensed the Holy Spirit saying – "Do more boats!" I again got paint and went to the waterfront to paint the next boat. By the end of the week the boats were painted and I had the joy of buying the paint and doing the labor. Of course, word had spread through the village about what the "Americano" was doing.

Evidently, they had not experienced someone serving them in this manner before. I was even invited one afternoon by the mayor of the village to come to his shelter on the shore and eat fish being cooked over an open fire. It appeared to me that he was honoring me by including me in his small circle of special friends who ate and drank together. It was an incredible time of connecting with the respected leaders of the area.

Later, I noticed one more boat that had not been painted, it was a small one, but I felt compelled to do it. As I was painting it, the owner came up to me and asked me in broken English – "Why are you doing this?" My only response was, "I love Jesus Christ and want to share His love."

It was encouraging to our team to see the favor God had given us through the many opportunities for serving the people and then later sharing Jesus as Savior. It was another "life-lesson" regarding the importance of humility and following the gentleness of our Master.

Personal Reflection: Do you find it a joy or chore to serve others? Is there someone in need that the Lord has brought to you that He wants you to humbly serve, without seeking recognition or reward? Will you do it for Jesus? The Holy Spirit can enlighten you as to how to be most effective in ministry through demonstrating the virtue of meekness. Be open and obedient to what He reveals. Give the glory to God, which shows true humility.

SELF-CONTROL

The Greek word is "egkrateia" (Strong's 1466/1468) and means "self-control, temperance, strong in a thing, to exercise self-restraint".

When we examine this attribute of the Holy Spirit's work in the believer, we need to focus on the aspect of temperance.

Involved in the virtue of temperance we discover the element of being "tempered". So, it's important to ask, "What does it mean to be tempered?"

If we use the example of tempered steel, we readily recognize that it has to do with strength that comes from testing. Steel becomes "tempered" when it is put in the fire until it becomes red-hot, then pounded to be shaped, then put in water to cool.

The process is repeated a number of times until the finished product is produced. The illustration of a village blacksmith making tools, comes to mind.

Temperance is a process and sometimes a very painful one. But, it can be productive in a person's life. The Holy Spirit can use times of testing or going through the fire, to make us strong in character. In light of the many temptations we face every day, this attribute is essential to living out the will of God and not allowing sin to hinder us. We are tested when tempted.

Out of the process of being tempered comes the ability to exercise self-restraint with the help of the Holy Spirit. This doesn't mean that we won't wrestle with turning away from temptations when they come before us repeatedly. Look at the Apostle Paul and what he shares in Romans 7:15, 24-25a (NIV):

> *"I do not understand what I do. For what I want to do I do not do, but what I hate I do...What a wretched man I am! Who will rescue me from this body of death? Thanks be to God -- through Jesus Christ our Lord!"*

We can all identify with him. There are times when we think we are doing so well, having victory in our walk with Jesus, and a temptation takes us off guard and we give in. This is an on-going challenge. The Holy Spirit wants us to learn and grow through each struggle, not give up and give in.

Jesus said to His disciples in the Garden of Gethsemane, when they fell asleep while He was praying – *"Keep watching and praying that you may not enter into temptation; the spirit is willing, but the flesh is weak."* (Matthew 26:41). These men had been with Jesus over three years and should have been tempered enough by now to endure. In reality, they had a long way to go. The greatest test was yet to come and when it did, they all ran!

Jesus calls each of us as His followers to be alert and be praying, asking the Holy Spirit to help us deal with temptation so it doesn't deal with us.

Someone once said, "Sin will always take you farther than you want to go and cost you more than you want to pay!". How true that is.

One day when I went to the mailbox and pulled out the mail there was a large catalog. The company's name across the top of the magazine was *Victoria's Secret*.

The picture of the woman on the front cover revealed what I needed to do with it – toss it! I did, without looking further and told Vivian when she came home later. I didn't need this temptation to interfere with my thoughts and relationship with my wife. I believe the Holy Spirit was helping me and cheering me on.

There are various types of temptations we each face, where we need to demonstrate temperance and self-restraint. Here are some areas of challenge to our flesh:

■ **Visual** – What we view on TV, in movies, or on the internet can present temptations to sin. Also pictures that are texted to us from others. Then, there are books and magazines that can lead us to think thoughts that are immoral. Sometimes, just the magazine rack in the grocery store check-out can get our mind focused on sensual matters. We must guard our eyes and avoid what's presented.

- **Physical** – The temptation to apply inappropriate touch of a sexual nature or intent is giving in to sin. It will lead further and further into sin and be very destructive. This uncontrolled behavior has ruined the lives of many children, youth, and adults. In our culture today, couples living together unmarried has become acceptable, even among those who claim to be Christ-followers. Sadly, they have given in to temptation and are living in sin before God and others. Hebrews 13:4 gives a strong warning against this.

- **Language** -- We are very aware of what James tells us about the power of the tongue and the end result. If we do not temper or control our tongue and show self-restraint, there may be cursing, gossip, slander, lying, belittling, rudeness, and the like that comes forth. If you find yourself involved in any of these sins, it is crucial to ask the Holy Spirit to search your heart to reveal what is causing this to happen.

- **Emotions** – What happens when anger, jealousy, envy, pride, intimidating, and controlling behaviors are evident in our relationships? This is a serious indication that the Holy Spirit is not being allowed to work and help the person become Christ-like.

- **Mind or Will** -- We have a choice in all we do...how we spend the money we have or don't have (such as credit card use), how much and what types of foods we eat, how much and what TV programs we watch, what video or computer games we play and how long we play them. Then there are the addictions to drugs (both illegal or prescription drugs), alcohol, gambling, pornography, computer usage, hobbies, recreation, sports, etc. Where we spend our time and resources reveals a lot about what controls our lives. We must look in the mirror and address what's going on before it becomes out of control and does damage.

The book of Proverbs in the Old Testament has much to say on a person's behavior. I'd encourage you to read a chapter a day for the next month and see what the Holy Spirit reveals to you. There are words of wisdom and words of warning. Keep a daily journal and write down those areas where you need God's help in order to have victory.

God loves us too much to see us self-destruct. We must keep watching and praying continually, allowing the Holy Spirit to do His work, His way.

It's always to our benefit to examine the negative examples recorded in Scripture that serve as a warning to us. We can learn from the mistakes of others and not make them ourselves. We discover the consequences of lack of self-control or self-restraint at the very beginning of humanity. Check these out these two crucial situations.

Genesis 3:6 -- Adam and Eve knew God's command, but chose not to restrain themselves. We discover that:

> *"When the woman saw that the tree was good for food, and that it was a delight to the eyes, and that the tree was desirable to make one wise, she took from its fruit and ate; and she gave also to her husband with her, and he ate."*

How often do we disobey God by going after something that is a *"delight to the eyes"* or *"desirable"* to our mind?

When we partake of whatever it is that God has warned us against, we find out the negative impact it has on us and our relationship with Him. It is not good and leads us away from God, if not confessed and changed.

Sin always breaks fellowship with God – that's a dangerous place to be. Repentance restores our relationship to God (see I John 1:9).

Genesis 4:5b-8 – The offspring of Adam and Eve were infected with the sin of their parents. Sin had entered humanity. The second great tragedy took place after God accepted Abel's offering and not Cain's offering. Scripture tells us:

> *"...So Cain became very angry and his countenance fell. Then the Lord said to Cain, 'Why are you angry? And why has your*

*countenance fallen? If you do well, will not your
countenance be lifted up? And if you do not do
well, sin is crouching at the door; and its desire
is for you, but you must master it."*

The older brother, Cain, is jealous. He gets angry and
depressed. God comes to warn him in love, but he chooses
to turn from God and act on his sinful emotions. The Lord
shows him what is going on and what he must do.

But, instead of obeying and getting right with God, he
takes matters into his own hands and makes the situation
worse. The result? Murder! How Adam and Eve must
have cried when this evil act became known.

God told Cain that sin's *"desire is for you, but you
must master it."* In other words, he was to use self-control
so that sin's destructive force would not happen.

God has given each of us a free-will and the dignity of
responsibility. We are not robots or puppets on a string –
we can choose to obey or disobey.

Henry and Richard Blackaby give the following insight
regarding anger. They state:

"Few things are more destructive to Christians
than anger. Anger causes us to lose our self-
control and to say and do things we would
otherwise never consider. Anger, if allowed to
remain, turns into bitterness that eats away at our
hearts...Anger does not bring about God's

redemptive work; far more often it hinders what God is working to accomplish." [11]

Anger causes us to act without sound reason and rational, which results in the loss of self-control. It turns into bitterness that eats away at our hearts and ruins relationships. This is serious! The Holy Spirit is in us as believers to warn us and help us deal with any anger, jealousy, bitterness, or other infections of sin in our lives. It's for our good and God's glory.

As a pastor, I realize the need to have one or more accountability partners. For me, these are other men who can check in on me with regard to how I'm handling temptation. Because they care, they ask the hard, but important "accountability" questions. They want to see me succeed and be victorious in my personal life, marriage, family, and ministry. They are watching my back, where Satan likes to ambush me. I can also go to these men and own up when I've given in. They don't condemn me, they pray with and for me. God has used committed servants to keep me on the *"...paths of righteousness for His name's sake."* (Psalm 23:3). What a blessing they are.

Why not ask the Holy Spirit to show you one or more individuals that He can use to strengthen or temper you in your spiritual walk. They will be a great blessing to you.

Keep in mind from day to day the words the Lord put on the heart of Moses just prior to his death. He called the people of Israel to walk in obedience to the Lord declaring:

"See, I have set before you today life and prosperity, and death and adversity; in that I command you today to love the LORD your God, to walk in His ways and to keep His commandments...that the LORD your God may bless you...". (Deuteronomy 30:15-16)

We must continually and conscientiously choose *"life and prosperity"*. This must be intentional.

We make many choices each day of our life, let's allow the Holy Spirit to help us walk out our love and faith in Jesus by turning away from temptation and sin.

Personal Reflection: Reflect for a moment on your own life right now. What is your greatest area of temptation? Are you demonstrating self-restraint? Is the Holy Spirit developing temperance in you? If you are giving in to temptation, how is Satan using this to hinder your closeness to the Lord and witness to others?

Keep In Step With The Spirit!

After the apostle Paul identifies the fruit of the Holy Spirit, he concludes with the admonition, *"Since we live by the Spirit, let us keep in step with the Spirit."* (Galatians 5:25 NIV). Every true believer has the Holy Spirit in them, but not every believer is *"in step"* with the Spirit.

Unfortunately, I meet people like this all the time. I often ask – "What's wrong with this picture?" Their talk and walk don't line up with God's Word, which is His will for all of us. I can't change anyone else, only myself. Full submission to the Lord is what makes the difference in one's life.

When the Apostle Paul challenges us to *"keep in step"*, he is using a very familiar military analogy. Those of Paul's day were used to seeing Roman soldiers marching from one place to another. They marched *"in step"* as a troop. Sometimes the commander may shout out, "Right, left, right, left…" just to keep the soldiers in line as they marched. If one soldier got out of step, it became very obvious and embarrassing. In fact, it messed up the marching order. You get the point.

The literal Greek translation of this phrase, used by Paul is, "walk in line with". In other words, we are to be so devoted to the will and work of God that we submit to the Holy Spirit in every area of our lives. We then follow His leading so the result is walking "in line with" Him.

As pointed out previously, sin causes us to get out of line with the Spirit and affects our fruitfulness. Anne Graham Lotz points out:

"There is one primary "internal blight" that attacks the branches of the Vine, which, if not severely dealt with, will destroy our fruitfulness. The "blight" is sin. Sin obstructs the free flow of the "sap" of the Holy Spirit in our lives. And since the Holy Spirit is the One Who truly produces the fruit that we bear, anything that grieves or quenches Him affects our fruitfulness." [12]

I agree with the insight shared in The Life Application Bible notes (Galatians 5:22) regarding the way to mature the fruit of the Holy Spirit in us. It explains the following:

"If we want the fruit of the Spirit to develop in our lives, we must recognize that all of these characteristics are found in Christ. Thus the way to grow them is to join our lives to his (see John 15:4). We must know him, love him, remember him, imitate him. The result will be that we will fulfill the intended purpose of the law – loving God and man." [13]

The Holy Spirit knows what's best for us. Let's keep marching *"in step"* with Him to magnify Jesus Christ, our spiritual Commander-in-Chief!

Chapter 7 – The Ministry Gifts of the Spirit

We've already discovered the unique ways the Holy Spirit worked during the Old Testament by imparting a specific anointing on individuals at distinct times.

In the New Testament, after Jesus imparted the Holy Spirit upon His disciples after His resurrection (John 20:22), we see an expanded work of the Spirit in the lives of believers.

This is evident in the specific "gifts" given. These spiritual gifts are from Jesus to His followers through the internal work of the Spirit.

The Apostle Peter clarifies the importance of the spiritual gifts for us:

"As each one has received a special gift, employ it in serving one another as good stewards of the manifold grace of God. Whoever speaks, is to do so as one who is speaking the utterances of God; whoever serves, is to do so as one who is serving by the strength which God supplies; so that in all things God may be glorified through Jesus Christ, to whom belongs the glory and dominion forever and ever. Amen." (I Peter 4:10-11)

We each have a *"special gift"* to be used in God's work.

Note carefully the reason for the impartation of spiritual gifts – *"...serving one another as good stewards of the manifold grace of God"*. We have the privilege of administering God's grace into the lives of others. We need to always keep in mind that the gifts are not about us. They are about God and what He wants to do through us to impact others and fulfill His purposes on the earth.

As servants of Jesus (Romans 1:1) we are to seek to serve one another and bring God glory in the process.

Dr. John Maxwell, in the <u>Maxwell Leadership</u> <u>Bible</u>, points out that in I Peter 4:10-11, there are five observations about our spiritual gift(s):

1. Every one of us has at least one spiritual gift (v. 10).

2. Spiritual gifts are intended to serve people, not bolster our reputations (v. 10).

3. We use our gifts as stewards, not owners (v. 10).

4. God is the source and the sustainer of every gift (v. 11).

5. We are to employ our gifts as though we were serving the Lord (v. 11). [1]

Maxwell also shares three negative results that occur when we do not use our gift properly. These results are:

1. We are disobedient.

2. The Body of Christ suffers.

3. God is not glorified. [2]

From what the Bible reveals, we should acknowledge the significance of spiritual gifts and their purpose in Jesus' plan for His Church. Let's explore these gifts of the Spirit further.

I like to put the spiritual gifts into three categories. They are as follows:

■ **Ministry Gifts** – Ephesians 4:11-12

■ **Motivational Gifts** – Romans 12:3-8;
   I Corinthians 12:28

■ **Manifestation Gifts** – I Corinthians 12-14

Each category of spiritual gifts reveal God's specific work that is designed to bring Him glory. Let's first examine the "Ministry Gifts".

Ministry Gifts

In Ephesians 4:11-12, we have identified distinct "callings" in ministry by the Holy Spirit from Jesus. These involve different leadership roles and responsibilities. These are not as common to the body of Christ as the other gifts of the Spirit are. They are for a certain number of individuals who serve as leaders in ministry.

Scripture reveals, *"And He gave some as apostles, and some as prophets, and some as evangelists, and some as pastors and teachers."* (v. 11). The Apostle Paul further points out that these gifts are *"for the equipping of the saints for the work of service, to the building up of the body of Christ."* (v. 12).

These specific leaders have an on-going challenge that can only be fully accomplished through the power and leading of the Holy Spirit. This *"equipping"* of Christ-followers is a process that at times can be discouraging and over-whelming. Leaders must keep looking to Jesus in fulfilling their responsibilities and must rely completely on the work of the Holy Spirit in and through them.

The Spirit Filled Life Bible gives more details on each of these appointments or callings as imparted by Jesus Christ. Jerry Horner, the New Testament Editor, explains the following:

"The five ministry offices listed here are gifts that Christ gave for the nurture and equipping of His church, not for hierarchical control or ecclesiastical competition. Beyond the distinct role filled by the original founding apostles, the NT mentions enough additional apostles to indicate that this office, with that of prophets, is as continuing a ministry in the church as the more commonly acknowledged offices of evangelists, pastors, and teachers (some make pastor-teacher one office). There is no prescribed formula or "gift-mix" for any particular office, as God uses different people in different ways in each of these five ministries Christ has given. Uniqueness is manifested in individuals according to the varied gifts God the Father has given them (Rom. 12:3-8) and joined with whatever gifts the Holy Spirit distributes to or through them (I Cor. 12:4-11). The distinct gifts of the Father (Rom. 12), the Son (Eph. 4), and the Spirit (I Cor. 12) ought not to be confused, nor should any of the five ministry offices in this text be limited to the operation of any particular gift."[3]

The specific gifts revealed in Ephesians 4:11, can be identified as the "Gifts of the Son – To Facilitate and Equip the Body of the Church".[4]

Let's examine the following explanations given by Paul Walker in the Spirit Filled Life Bible:

1. APOSTLES

a. In apostolic days referred to a select group chosen to carry out directly the ministry of Christ; including the assigned task given to a few to complete the sacred canon of the Holy Scriptures.

b. Implies the exercise of a distinct representative role of broader leadership given by Christ.

c. Functions as a messenger or spokesman of God.

d. In contemporary times refers to those who have the spirit of apostleship in remarkably extending the work of the church, opening fields to the gospel, and overseeing larger sections of the body of Jesus Christ.

2. PROPHET

a. A spiritually mature spokesman/proclaimer with a special, divinely focused message to the church or the world.

b. A person uniquely gifted at times with insight into future events.

3. EVANGELIST

   a. Refers primarily to a special gift of preaching or witnessing in a way that brings unbelievers into the experience of salvation.

   b. Functionally, the gift of evangelist operates for the establishment of new works, while pastors and teachers follow up to organize and sustain.

   c. Essentially, the gift of evangelist operates to establish converts and to gather them spiritually and literally into the body of Christ.

4. PASTORS AND TEACHER

   a. The word "pastor" comes from a root meaning "to protect", from which we get the word "shepherd".

   b. Implies the function of a shepherd/leader to nurture, teach, and care for the spiritual needs of the body. [5]

For clarification, I would comment that the ministry gift of "apostles" refers originally to those who saw Jesus Christ alive after His resurrection, which includes eleven of the original disciples and later Saul, who became the Apostle Paul.

I believe that in the time period after the death of these original Apostles, the "spirit of apostleship" continues to fulfill this work of God. I would include individuals who plant churches and oversee them, as well as missionaries who go into new regions to begin new works for the Gospel of Christ. These are "sent out ones" fulfilling the work of God until Jesus returns.

I have encountered those in ministry who have been identified as apostles by their fellowship and serve together with other apostles in ministering to a variety of churches as they travel to different areas. I respect and honor their service to Jesus and His Church and would commend them for being obedient to serve where they feel led by the Holy Spirit.

Regarding another of the ministry gifts, numerous Bible scholars combine "pastors and teachers" into one distinct calling. This is because of the Greek grammatical construction of the text. It would also follow that one called to be a pastor must also be qualified and capable to teach. Paul's instruction to Timothy confirms this:

> *"The elders who rule well are to be considered worthy of double honor, especially those who work hard at preaching and teaching."* (I Timothy 5:17)

The NIV Study Bible explains in the footnotes regarding this calling (Ephesians 4:11): *"pastors and teachers* – Because of the Greek grammatical construction (also, the word "some" introduces both words together), it is clear that these groups of gifted people are closely related. Those who have pastoral care for God's people (the image of shepherding) will naturally provide "food" from the Scriptures (teaching). They will be especially gifted as teachers (cf. I Ti 3:2)." [6]

5. TEACHERS

I want to add "teachers" to the ministry gifts and separate them as a fifth "calling" because it is evident in the body of Christ that there are those with this distinct leadership gift. They are not serving as pastor of a congregation but lead on a national or international level as teachers.

As I look at various ministry roles and an explanation of what they entail, certain people come to my mind. The people I'll be naming are well-known individuals, but these ministry gifts are evident in whomever Jesus chooses to entrust them to. Here are some leaders under each of the distinct types of ministry gifts to give you a connection:

- **Apostles (spirit of apostleship):** Loren Cunningham, who began Youth With A Mission; Pat Robertson, who began The Christian Broadcasting Network (CBN) and Regent University in Virginia Beach, Virginia; Franklin Graham, who began The Samaritan's Purse ministry with Operation Christmas Child and other compassion ministries.

167

- **Prophets (and Prophetess):** David Wilkerson, who served Times Square Church in New York City; Dr. Peter Wagner, associated with Fuller Theological Seminary; Jane Hansen of Aglow International; Cindy Jacobs of Generals of Intercession; Peter Helms of YWAM; and Dutch Sheets, who operates in this ministry gifting world-wide.

- **Evangelists:** The most well-known of those with this ministry gift and calling is Dr. Billy Graham, of the Billy Graham Evangelistic Association, as well as Franklin Graham, his son. Also Luis Palau, of the Luis Palau Evangelistic Ministry and Greg Laurie, of Harvest Ministries, that sponsors Harvest Crusades. These are just a few.

- **Pastors-Teachers:** Some of the well-known pastors who have local and national impact in the United States are: Chuck Swindoll, David Jeremiah, Rick Warren, Bill Hybels, Charles Stanley, Andy Stanley, John Hagee, Matt Chandler, Ed Young Jr. Jim Cymbala, and Jack Hayford. There are thousands of others who serve in smaller congregations. These individuals play a very significant part in touching people's lives in a personal manner.

- **Teachers:** There are numerous teachers that impact many people through their ministry. Among them are Beth Moore, Lee Stroble, Francis Chan, Ron

Boehme, John Maxwell, Perry Stone, and Joyce Meyer to name a few.

Each of these servants has been called to reach, equip, and prepare the followers of Jesus Christ, helping them develop and mature to serve God's purposes.

I have personally been called by Jesus to be a Pastor-Teacher.

I can recall the exact place and words the Holy Spirit spoken into my heart – "You will be preaching Jesus the rest of your life!" This took place in Shenandoah National Park, Virginia.

As a sophomore in college, I had applied to serve as an assistant to the Student Minister in the program, "A Christian Ministry in the National Parks".

When the letter of acceptance came to me, it congratulated me on being chosen as the Student Minister. I began realizing that the Lord had something more for me than what I planned. My personal calling came just prior to leading the worship service in the amphitheatre in Matthew's Arm Campground one Sunday morning at 8:30 a.m. That's when I heard the Holy Spirit speak. I have held on to that clear call from God during difficult times in pastoral ministry and it has given me the conviction to press on and persevere in serving Christ as a pastor.

The Lord has been faithful in allowing me to serve in five different churches up to this point. They have each been very unique and of different denominations. It has been His call where He has led and when. He is Sovereign.

Do you sense Jesus is calling you to serve Him in one of these specific areas of ministry? It would be good to ask those who know and observe you, if they see you operating in one of these roles of leadership. The Holy Spirit continues to fulfill the will of Jesus in calling and developing specific people for specific ministry worldwide.

If you are already serving in one of these ministry callings, do it humbly. The gift is from God and has been entrusted to you. You are accountable to Him for how you use it.

Be fully submitted to Jesus in every aspect of ministry – *"as good stewards of the manifold grace of God"* (I Peter 4:10).. He must be Lord of your life and evident in your calling. Thank Him for the privilege of serving Him in this manner and for the opportunity to bring Him glory.

Chapter 8 – The Motivational Gifts of the Spirit

In Romans 12:6-8, the Apostle Paul informs believers of other various gifts that operate within the body of Christ. Whereas the "ministry gifts" are for ministry leaders to equip the Church, the "motivational gifts" are for all believers.

Each believer has one or more motivational gift. It is different from a natural talent we are born with or may develop, but may coincide closely. This is a spiritual gift given by the Holy Spirit after a person becomes a Christ-follower.

It is crucial for every believer to recognize God's work in his or her life. Paul makes an important statement prior to identifying these various gifts. He points out:

"For through the grace given me I say to everyone among you not to think more highly of himself than he ought to think; but to think so as to have sound judgment, as God has allotted to each a measure of faith. For just as we have many members in one body and all the members do not all have the same function, so we, who are

many are one body in Christ, and individually members one of another. (Romans 12:3-5).

This keeps the operation of spiritual gifts in proper perspective. We receive the gift(s) by God's grace. We are to operate in each gift with humility. We are all part of Christ's body. We do not all have the same function but are equally significant.

The Holy Spirit must be grieved when a person flaunts their spiritual gift as being more important that someone else's gift. He is the One who distributes the gifts to those whom the Father reveals. What are we saying to God when we think of ourselves as being better or *"more highly"* gifted (Romans 12:3)?

There are different gifts imparted to different people for different functions – all within Christ's Church. In light of this reality, we should each discover, develop, and distribute our gift or gifts.

Books and manuals have been written on just these specific spiritual gifts and there are on-line surveys that can be taken to help a person identify which gift or gifts they have. I believe a brief description of the motivational gifts is sufficient for our study regarding Holy Spirit convergence.

Dr. John Maxwell, in the Maxwell Leadership Bible, has defined each spiritual gift presented in Romans 12 with the following details.

1. ***Gift of Prophecy:*** to challenge others by declaring God's truth and calling for action.

2. ***Gift of Service or Ministry:*** to serve others and meet their needs.

3. ***Gift of Teaching:*** to explain truth so that others can understand and apply it.

4. ***Gift of Exhortation:*** to encourage, strengthen, and inspire others to be their best.

5. ***Gift of Giving:*** to generously share what God has given.

6. ***Gift of Leadership:*** to govern and oversee others so that the group moves forward.

7. ***Gift of Mercy:*** to empathize with, cheer, and show compassion to those who hurt. [1]

In I Corinthians 12:27-28, the Apostle Paul gives a summarization of different gifts. In verse 28, he includes "helps" and "administrations", which truly are spiritual gifts that would fit under this classification of "motivational gifts". I'll add these two gifts with my own personal understanding and definition of what they involve:

8. *Gift of Helps:* to assist in a specific area of ministry and help complete a task.

9. *Gift of Administrations:* to be able to coordinate, organize, maintain order, and delegate responsibilities.

Maxwell comments that, "Every resource God provides should be in use. Every believer is a steward of the abilities he or she has been given. Every leader is a manager whose goal should be to maximize everyone's gift." [2]

It seems that some pastors have a tendency to micromanage or take on more than what the Lord would have them do. I've been guilty of this. While serving in various churches, I realized the importance of recognizing the spiritual gifts present and releasing ministry to committed and capable individuals. This has been done by developing "Ministry Teams".

First, the Elders identify what ministry teams are needed in the church fellowship. They pray about who is to be the Ministry Team Leader of each. This person is to be a member of the church and willing to accept responsibly. They actually function as a servant-leader or deacon/deaconess over their area of ministry. These leaders are appointed by the Elders if they also believe the Lord is calling them to serve in a specific area.

The Ministry Team Leader of each team then seeks the leading of the Holy Spirit in contacting others, both members and non-members of the church, to serve with them.

They build their team by inviting others to take part in the ministry areas.

These teams provide a solid and stable foundation along with the Elders. The Elders then delegate ministry responsibilities to the various teams so gifted people can meet the need and function as the Holy Spirit has equipped them. This is a practical application of Ephesians 4:12. It is also following the example of what took place in Acts 6:1-6 when there was a specific need in the Jerusalem church.

The Apostles realized that Jesus wanted to use gifted people in His Church as it expanded and needs increased. These servant-leaders were to be *"full of the Holy Spirit and wisdom"* (Acts 6:3 NIV).

In the current church I am serving, Lighthouse Christian Church, the Elders have established six Ministry Teams. They are: Outreach, Education, Facility, Finance, Worship, and Hospitality. There are both men and women leading each team, bringing glory to the Lord and order in the church fellowship. Where appropriate, I, as Pastor or an Elder will serve on one or more of the teams.

The Spirit Filled Life Bible also identifies these gifts found in Romans 12:3-8, as "Gifts of the Father – Basic Life Purpose and Motivation". [3]

I believe it will be helpful to share the explanations given in the Spirit Filled Life Bible for clearer under-standing and practical application. This is in addition to what John Maxwell described previously. These are the following:

1. **PROPHECY**

    a. To speak with forthrightness and insight, especially when enabled by the Spirit of God (Joel 2:28).

    b. To demonstrate moral boldness and un-compromising commitment to worthy values.

    c. To influence others in one's arena of influence with a positive spirit of social or spiritual righteousness.

2. **MINISTRY**

    a. To minister and render loving, general service to meet the needs of others.

    b. Illustrated in the work and office of the deacon (Matthew 20:26).

3. **TEACHING**

    a. The supernatural ability to explain and apply the truths received from God for the church.

    b. Presupposes study and the Spirit's illumination providing the ability to make divine truth clear to the people of God.

c. Considered distinct from the work of the prophet who speaks as the direct mouth-piece of God.

4. EXHORATION

a. Literally means to call aside for the purpose of making an appeal.

b. In a broader sense it means to entreat, comfort, or instruct (Acts 4:36; Hebrews 10:25).

5. GIVING

a. The essential meaning is to give out of a spirit of generosity.

b. In a more technical sense it refers to those with resources aiding those without such resources (2 Corinthians 8:2; 9:11-13).

c. This gift is to be exercised without outward show or pride and with liberality (2 Corinthians 1:12; 8:2; 9:11,13).

6. LEADERSHIP

a. Refers to the one "standing in front."

b. Involves the exercise of the Holy Spirit in modeling, superintending, and developing the body of Christ.

c. To be exercised with diligence.

7. MERCY

a. To feel sympathy with the misery of another.

b. To relate to others in empathy, respect, and honesty.

c. To be effective, this gift is to be exercised with kindness and cheerfulness – not as a matter of duty. [4]

In regards to the motivational gifts, I've discovered that the Holy Spirit has entrusted me with more than one motivational gift for ministry. My "gift mix" or spiritual DNA consists of prophecy, leadership, exhortation, and teaching. The Lord has used each of these in different contexts of ministry over the years, both in pastoral roles and as director of Christian ministries.

You may operate in one gift or have more than one. Remember they come by God's grace and each serve to fulfill His plan through you.

In case you are not sure what gift(s) you have been given, consider these questions on each of these motivational gifts. Your answers may help you determine what the Lord has entrusted to you through the impartation of the Holy Spirit. Examine each and see what stands out as identifying your spiritual DNA.

- **Prophecy** – Do you feel God prompting you to share matters of truth and challenge others to take part in what God is revealing? Have you or are you doing this in some aspect of ministry?

- **Service or Ministry** – Do you find joy and fulfillment in serving others on either a small or large scale? Do you look for ways to serve others or be of help when needed? Do you readily volunteer to help with a need?

- **Teaching** – Do you enjoy doing research on a topic or Scripture, then develop the information and impart it to others? Does the discovery of new information excite you and motivate you to share it with others? Do others seem to grasp and respond to what you are teaching them?

- **Exhortation** – Do you build others up and inspire them to grow spiritually? Do you give counsel or disciple others in what is best for them? Do people seek you out for spiritual advice? Are people receptive to your advice and apply it?

- **Giving** – Do you find yourself joyfully sharing finances or material things with others? Are you often led to give your resources away to those in need or to specific ministries? Do you give things away even out of your own need at times?

- **Leadership** – Do you find yourself drawn to lead a group or team of people in a specific area of ministry? Do you accept and handle well the challenges that go with leading others? Do other people respond to and follow your leadership? Do you have a vision for leading a ministry and if so, are you able to implement it successfully?

- **Mercy** – Do you reach out to people in special caring ways, beyond praying for them? Is your heart drawn to people who are struggling, such as those in the hospital, shut-ins, lonely, or disadvantaged in some way?

- **Helps** – Do you get personally involved in practical work assignments? Do you enjoy being part of a support team? Are you cooperative and willing to complete the tasks assigned to you?

- **Administrations** – Do you like to organize and put things in order? Does it give you fulfillment to complete a specific task on time? Are you able to delegate work to others to be accomplished? Are you able to work with a variety of people and keep them "on task"?

What conclusion have you come to? What would you identify as your "primary" motivational gift?

Is there any other gift or gifts the Lord has given you in your spiritual DNA?

Now for the crucial question – Are you currently applying or using your gift(s) for God's glory in His kingdom work?

Sometimes, there are exceptional situations when the Lord may lead you to be involved in an unusual circumstance. There were two specific times in my life when the "gift of giving" (not one of my gifts) was exercised.

The first was when I was earning my Masters degree at Regent University. A fellow-classmate had been severely burned in an auto accident and there was a need for funds to purchase a "burn-suit" to promote healing. On my way home after finding this out in class, I sensed the Holy Spirit was leading Vivian and I to give all we had in our savings. This was the amount needed for the special "burn suit".

I shared the situation with Vivian and after praying over it, we agreed and acted upon it. We had three small children at the time. Vivian was working at McDonald's and I was working evenings at United Postal Service (UPS) to cover our basic needs.

There was such joy in the giving. I could hardly wait to turn the check over to the professor, who would see that it was applied anonymously. This was a "God-thing" and Vivian and I were thankful to share in it. The Lord used this to bring encouragement and healing to my classmate and his family.

Another time this happened was over ten years later when Vivian and I left full-time ministry to be part of the Crossroads Discipleship Training School (CDTS) with YWAM. It was the year of our 25th wedding anniversary, which we celebrated while in the school. We had sent out support letters and raised enough for half the cost.

We knew we were to go and were committed to trusting God for the rest of the funds, in His time. After the Teaching Phase of the CDTS was over, the Outreach Phase was next. The Lord had not only met our expenses through financial support coming in, but there was an extra $500.00 provided. We were blessed!

As the time drew closer for the final confirmation of who was to go on Outreach, it became known that several students did not have enough funds to make it possible to go. When we were asked to pray for our classmates needs to be met, the Holy Spirit revealed that Vivian and I were to bless others with the extra the Lord had given us. We joyfully gave a check for $500.00 knowing that God would use that amount for others to fulfill the mission assignment He had given them.

There was great rejoicing when the offerings were counted and given to those in need.

The "gift of giving" may be exercised by those with limited financial means, as well as, with those who have been entrusted with much. All we have belongs to the Lord and it is a joy to let go and give to others as He specifically leads through the work of the Holy Spirit. It becomes a special convergence experience in our life.

The Lord has "gifted" us uniquely. When we discover and apply our gift or gifts, we are invigorated and fulfilled. It's one thing to know your spiritual DNA and another to be operating in it. This will impact the rest of your life.

For further help in this area go the following website: www.gifttest.org and take the simple test to see what you discover about yourself. Ask the Holy Spirit to guide you in using the gift(s) that He has imparted to you and let the convergence continue.

Chapter 9 – The Manifestation Gifts of the Spirit

Jesus gave specific instructions prior to His ascension back to the Father in Heaven. In Mark 16:15-18, He reveals what He intends His followers to do. Take a look at these "final" instructions:

> *"And He said to them, 'Go into all the world and preach the gospel to all creation. He who has believed and has been baptized shall be saved; but he who has disbelieved shall be condemned. These signs will accompany those who have believed: in My name they will cast out demons, they will speak with new tongues; they will pick up serpents, and if they drink any deadly poison, it will not hurt them; they will lay hands on the sick, and they will recover."*

Jesus made it clear that there would be supernatural activity happening through His followers as they went out to share the gospel. This is the work of the kingdom of

God. It is Jesus' work through the Holy Spirit in the lives of believers. It is a work of faith and obedience.

The writer of Hebrews confirms the importance of the Spirit's supernatural involvement in building Jesus' Church. Note what is recorded in Hebrews 2:3b-4:

"...After it was first spoken through the Lord, it was confirmed to us by those who heard, God also testifying with them, both by signs and wonders and by various miracles and the gifts of the Holy Spirit according to His own will."

We must ask the following crucial questions – "Is Jesus still building His Church through the work of the Holy Spirit today?"; "Is the Holy Spirit limited as to how, when, and where He can work prior to the return of Christ?"; "Does Jesus still work through the supernatural gifts described in Scripture?".

I ask these questions because the manifestation gifts are sometimes denied, hindered, or ignored among some believers and church fellowships today.

Some believe these "miracle" gifts ended with the death of the Apostle John, since the first century Church seemed to have been established at that point. I believe they continue today and will continue until Jesus comes back in glory. There is continual manifold evidence of this.

There are many great Christian leaders of the past and those living today that attest to God's continual work – *"both by signs and wonders and by various miracles and the gifts of the Holy Spirit...* ", since Pentecost. They are respected and credible servants of the Lord.

Among them is, Dr. Jack Hayford, Lead Pastor of The Church on the Way (Van Nuys, California), past president of The International Church of the Foursquare Gospel and current Chancellor of The King's University. He has written excellent books explaining the unique work of the Spirit in our time, as well as many songs we sing in worship, such as "Majesty". He is the General Editor of the Spirit Filled Life Bible, from which I have made numerous references to throughout this book.

There are also large denominations such as The Assemblies of God, International Church of the Foursquare Gospel, Church of God and other independent or non-denominational church fellowships that evidence the manifestation gifts through the Holy Spirit currently.

According to the Center for the Study of Global Christianity at the Gordon-Conwell Theological Seminary, over the last century, membership in churches that believe in the continuing work of the Holy Spirit as in the early Church, "has grown geometrically from less than 1 million to nearly 700 million..." [1]

That is an amazing increase in the past 100 years!

These are Christ-followers who have experienced or believe in the unique filling of the Holy Spirit, which is available after coming to faith in Jesus.

Believers baptized with the Holy Spirit after conversion have also experienced the Spirit imparting manifestation gifts to them at different times and in different places.

The Apostle Paul tells the body of Christ in I Corinthians 12:1(NIV) – *"Now about spiritual gifts, brothers, I do not want you to be ignorant."* He then continues explaining the importance of these manifestation gifts.

I've discovered in my years of ministry that people are often afraid of what they don't understand or can't figure out in their rational mind. God calls us to walk in faith and not fear.

There are mysteries with God and His ways that we will never understand or figure out, yet we are to trust Him. These mysteries are beyond our intellect. We have already seen evidence in the Old and New Testament of the Spirit's peculiar ways of working, so it shouldn't alarm us.

I believe these gifts are to be accepted and acted on by faith in God, who does the supernatural work. It is His work, but we get to participate in it.

Before we examine the specific manifestation gifts revealed in Scripture, let's get a better understanding of what God intends for us to know, so we are not ignorant or un-informed.

First, what does Paul teach us about these unique gifts?

- ■ **I Corinthians 12:4** – *"Now there are varieties of gifts, but the same Spirit."*

The Holy Spirit is the One who imparts whatever manifestation gift that is revealed.

188

- ■ **I Corinthians 12:7** – *"But to each one is given the manifestation of the Spirit for the common good."*

The purpose of the impartation or manifestation is to edify and build up believers. Jesus wants to encourage His people through the use of these gifts in His Church.

- ■ **I Corinthians 12:11** – *"But one and the same Spirit works all these things, distributing to each one individually just as He wills."*

It is clear the Spirit is in control and He determines what is going to take place. God must receive the glory for whatever occurs through the manifestation that happens. It is His work as He wills.

- ■ **I Corinthians 13:1-2** – *"If I speak with the tongues of men and of angels, but do not love, I have become a noisy gong or a clanging cymbal. If I have the gift of prophecy, and know all mysteries and all knowledge; and if I have all faith, so as to remove mountains, but do not have love, I am nothing."*

This puts the operation of the gifts in perspective – God's perspective. Love for God and love for others must be our motivation. If love is missing, then application is out of order. We can't miss this!

- **I Corinthians 14:1** – *"Pursue love, yet desire earnestly spiritual gifts, especially that you may prophesy."*

As followers of Jesus, we should be open and eager to be used by Him through the manifestation of the Spirit. Paul calls the body of Christ to "earnestly" desire God to work through the miraculous gifts.

- **I Corinthians 14:12** – *"So also you, since you are zealous of the spiritual gifts, seek to abound for the edification of the church."*

Build up, edify, encourage – these are the emphasis of the manifestation gifts of the Spirit. We must always check our spirit to make sure that we are operating under the direction of the Holy Spirit.

Pastors and leaders are to discern this when someone senses the Holy Spirit is leading them. If whatever happens does not bring edification, then this must be addressed and lovingly corrected. This is an important responsibility of leadership.

The matter of being *"zealous of the spiritual gifts"* appears to be lacking in many fellowships today. What's this revealing about our worship and ministry?

- **I Corinthians 14:32-33** – *"and the spirits of prophets are subject to prophets; for God is not a*

God of confusion but of peace, as in all the churches of the saints."

Regretfully, some have not operated under Godly control and matters got out of control. People are confused instead of encouraged when this happens. In some situations, a person's emotions may override the leading of the Spirit and matters are carried to an extreme. God works in the balance – He is a God of order, not confusion.

When the manifestation gifts are exercised according to God's Word, then God's order is followed and there is peace. The peace that results is an indication of the Presence of the Lord in the *"churches of the saints"*.

I find it a true delight to be among God's forgiven people – His saints. I don't want to dishonor the Lord in any way. My passion is to let God have His way and not stand in the way of the Holy Spirit's work.

■ **I Corinthians 14:40** – *"But all things must be done properly and in an orderly manner."*

The *"orderly manner"* referred to here is what the Apostle Paul reveals previously in verses 26-33. Look at the specific instructions given here. There is no place for confusion when the Holy Spirit is truly at work and leading among God's people.

I want to re-emphasize the foundational matter of operating in any of the gifts by sincere love. The <u>Spirit Filled Life Bible</u> "Kingdom Dynamics", points out:

"Since the basis of all gifts is love, that spirit of love is the qualifying factor for Biblical exercise of the gifts of the Holy Spirit. Thus, those in authority must 'try the spirits' to assure that those who exercise spiritual gifts actually 'follow after love' as well as 'desire spiritual gifts'." [2]

May the Holy Spirit Himself convict us if we ever neglect to operate out of love!

Understanding the Manifestation Gifts

It is helpful to divide the manifestation gifts into three categories. They are the following:

1. **REVELATION GIFTS** – the power to <u>know</u> as enabled by the Spirit.

2. **POWER GIFTS** – the power to <u>do</u> as enabled by the Spirit.

3. **EXHORTATION GIFTS** – the power to <u>speak truth</u> as enabled by the Spirit.

It is important to acknowledge that other believers in the body of Christ can exercise and administer God's grace through the manifestation of the Holy Spirit with a spiritual gift, not just pastors or ministry leaders. The Apostle Paul makes this known in I Corinthians 12:27-28:

"Now you are Christ's body, and individually members of it. And God has appointed in the church, first apostles, second prophets, third teachers, then miracles, then gifts of healing, helps, administrations, various kinds of tongues."

There is no mention of how long one has been a true believer before they may operate in the gifts. As we have seen before, the Spirit makes the determination of who He will use and when He will use them.

When I was serving in pastoral ministry at Horizon Church in Seattle, Washington, on occasion the Holy Spirit would move upon one of the children of the congregation. This child would be in Children's Church and share with a teacher what God was revealing to her. The teacher would then bring her up the Worship Center and have her share with the congregation about the revelation that God revealed to her. It was exciting to have this happen in our midst and of great encouragement to all present. The Lord uses children also to speak truth through the Holy Spirit.

He loves to surprise us!

The Manifestation of the "Revelation Gifts"

The Word of Wisdom
(I Corinthians 12:8)

This manifestation is also known as *"the message of wisdom"* (I Corinthians 12:8 NIV). The <u>Spirit Filled Life Bible</u> notes five aspects of the "Word of Wisdom":

A. Supernatural perspective to ascertain the divine means for accomplishing God's will in given situations.

B. Divinely given power to appropriate spiritual intuition in problem solving.

C. Sense of divine direction.

D. Being led by the Holy Spirit to act appropriately in a given set of circumstances.

E. Knowledge rightly applied: wisdom works interactively with knowledge and discernment. [3]

Fran Lance, in her book, <u>You Can Minister in the Spiritual Gifts</u>, shares the following insight regarding this gift:

"The word of wisdom is not the natural wisdom of man. It cannot be obtained by learning and becoming wise through the process of education. Rather, it is wisdom given supernaturally by the Holy Spirit at a particular time for a particular purpose." [4]

I've discovered that the Holy Spirit will often reveal specific matters regarding a city or area when believers do "Prayer-walking". He will show them what is going on in the spirit-realm. There are people committed to faithfully doing "Prayer-walks" around their neighborhood, community, city, or state. They pray as the Spirit directs them and imparts revelation to them.

Those involved in YWAM Outreaches often begin to minister in a new area by doing "Prayer-walks" to see what *"word of wisdom"* the Spirit may give them for proceeding. They go out in teams to pray, read Scripture, and declare God's blessing. During this time or at the end they share insights the Holy Spirit has impressed on them or revealed to them.

At one point in ministry, I was led by the Holy Spirit to divide up the city of Seattle into different sections, known as "Prayer- zones". I then prayed for Prayer Team Leaders, who would adopt a "zone" and gather a team of intercessors to walk, pray, and discern what the Holy Spirit was revealing. The reports that came in from the Prayer Team Leaders were amazing and "the message or word of wisdom" was received regarding what God wanted to do in each section.

When Vivian and I were YWAM Team Leaders during the Outreach Phase of our CDTS, there were several key times when we needed divine wisdom in what manner of ministry we were to proceed in. As the team went to prayer over this, the Spirit revealed to us what we were to do. One of these times *"the word of wisdom"* was that we were to leave a personal gift with the villagers as we came to the end of our time in the Philippines. As we continued to pray, the Spirit revealed we were to take an offering among our team and use the money to buy Bibles printed in the native Philippine language.

Our team was getting low on funds, but each person determined in their heart before God what they were to give toward this. The next day the money was collected and two team members made the long trip into Manila. At the Manila Bible Society they were able to purchase 50 Bibles. What a miracle! When they returned with the Bibles, the team was ecstatic. We were each able to give away Bibles to the people the Lord allowed us to build special relationships with during our time there.

When I went to my first home with a new Bible, a child met me at the door. The child understood English and I explained that I had a gift to give to the family before leaving to go back to the United States. The child told the parents and they came to the door. When I presented the Bible and they saw it was in their native language, they got tears in their eyes and the woman held it to her chest.

It was evident that this had great worth to them. They were so grateful to have their own copy of God's Word. It was a simple gift to give, but one that would impact their lives and future generations greatly through the Holy Spirit.

The Holy Spirit imparted wisdom to our team to accomplish God's work of salvation throughout that village. Other team members returned and shared similar experiences. We left the village two days later with great joy in our hearts as we sensed Jesus saying – mission accomplished!

<u>The Word of Knowledge</u>
(I Corinthians 12:8)

This is a specific revelation for a specific person or group. The message can come through a vision, a dream, or a prompting of the Spirit. It is information that the person had no prior knowledge of. It can be spoken spontaneously without any forethought. This is also known as *"the message of knowledge"* (I Corinthians 12:8 NIV).

The <u>Spirit Filled Life Bible</u> notes six aspects of the "Word of Knowledge":

A. Supernatural revelation of the divine will and plan.

B. Supernatural insight or understanding of circumstances or a body of facts by revelation: that is, without assistance of any human resource but solely by divine aid.

C. Implies a deeper and more advanced understanding of the communicated acts of God.

D. Involves moral wisdom for right living and relationships.

E. Requires objective understanding concerning divine things in human duties.

F. May also refer to knowledge of God or of the things that belong to God, as related in the gospel.[5]

For my Master of Biblical Studies thesis while at Regent University (Virginia Beach, Virginia), I chose to focus on "Healing Ministry Teams". These consisted of three to four people who would be available to pray over an individual to identify the root cause of a person's struggle.

Our family worshipped at Cornerstone Community Church in Virginia Beach at the time. I had opportunity to lead a "Healing Ministry Team" there. The purpose was to have the Holy Spirit reveal what was going on deep inside a person that contributed to the physical issue and have the person deal with that. There would be times that the Spirit would bring forth a *"word of knowledge"* revealing that there was un-forgiveness at the root of the problem or there was lack of trust in God due to a painful childhood experience.

The Holy Spirit, being God, knows what's going on in every person's life. As He revealed root issues, different people would pray and then the person would pray, seeking for Jesus to heal and restore them.

Also, while at Regent University, I was privileged to work for *The 700 Club* television ministry with Dr. Pat Robertson and various co-hosts. During the television program, when there would be a special time of inter-cession through prayer, either Pat or one of the co-hosts with him would receive a *"word of knowledge"* from the Holy Spirit.

They would simply speak out what the Spirit was revealing. It may have been the healing of someone's sight, arthritis, a tumor, or some other problem where God was doing a divine work. They would name the problem area and say – "God is touching this area of your body. You need to receive your healing in faith and thank Him for what He is doing."

People would be encouraged to call in and bear witness to this work of God in their life. Later, television broadcasts would be shown revealing how the Lord did indeed work His work through the *"word of knowledge"* spoken out on a prior telecast. This ministry of the Holy Spirit continues on the regular broadcast of *The 700 Club*.

I am always blessed watching and joining in this special time of prayer. You can watch the telecast on television or on the internet at: www.CBN.com, and can encourage others needing God's touch to watch it also.

There have been times in worship on a Sunday morning that during a song, the Holy Spirit will move upon my spirit and call me to be obedient to give a *"word or message of knowledge"* to the congregation when the song is finished. I don't know beforehand what I am to say, but completely trust the Spirit to give me the words of Jesus to His people.

The words that come forth are His message of love, encouragement, comfort, and assurance to His followers. Often, when I open my eyes and look upon the congregation afterward, I see tears in people's eyes. The Lord knows what we need and when we need it. He uses our submission to Him to bring forth what will touch the hearts of people for His glory.

Another experience in this manifestation of the Spirit came forth when I was teaching at Discovery Bay YWAM base near Port Townsend, Washington. The base director came to the front of the room after a time of worship in song and said, "God has given me a picture of us. We are all on a bicycle. Some don't like the one they are on. Ask the Lord to show you why you don't like the one you are on."

Each person in the Discipleship Training School (DTS) was challenged by this *"word of knowledge"* to seek the Lord on what He was specifically saying to them.

This gave the DTS leaders the opportunity to meet with the students later and have them share what was being revealed to them individually.

It is wonderful to see how the Spirit works in different ways to touch the lives of people and draw them closer to the Father and His Son, Jesus Christ.

Distinguishing between Spirits
(I Corinthians 12:10)

This gift is also identified as the *"discerning of spirits"* (I Corinthians 12:10 NKJV). We must note that the word "spirits" is plural, giving us the understanding that we need to determine which "spirit" is at work in a given situation. This gift is a supernatural revelation of the Holy Spirit to identify the presence of good or evil.

In I John 4:1-2, the Apostle John states, *"Beloved, do not believe every spirit, but test the spirits to see whether they are from God, because many false prophets have gone out into the world."*

Christians have been led astray in the past and still are. The Apostle Paul warns of being deceived and mentions those who have *"...suffered ship-wreck in regard to their faith. Among these are Hymenaeus and Alexander..."* (I Timothy 1:19-20a). The Holy Spirit is available to show us so we can choose wisely. He will reveal what spirit is at work in a given situation, whether an evil spirit, a person's misguided spirit, or a heavenly angelic spirit.

The Spirit Filled Life Bible reveals two aspects of this gift of *"discerning of spirits"*:

A. Supernatural power to detect the realm of the spirits and their activities.

B. Implies the power of spiritual insight – supernatural revelation of plans and purposes of the Enemy and his forces.[6]

Satan can act as a roaring lion seeking those to devour or he can appear as an angel of light to deceive many. The more we know the truth of God from the Word and Spirit of God, the harder it will be to be deceived by Satan. Remember, he will use whatever and whomever he can to lead people astray. Be on guard continually.

The Holy Spirit wants to help us discern anything that is not of God. There are masses of people today that are into "angel worship". They have adopted their own personal angel, have given the angel a name, and worship it. How tragic that a person can be so deceived!

There are also millions connected to the many cults and false religions in our world. They have believed *deceitful spirits and doctrines of demons"* (I Timothy 4:1b). This is to their eternal destruction. What a blessing it is to be a true child of God and have His light shining through us.

In the Philippines, while living in the small fishing village, our CDTS team discovered a facility not too far from where we stayed that had a sign, "The Church of the Living God". The sad thing was – the man leading the group claimed to be the living God! He was worshipped there by certain people in the village who wore white silk gowns as they attended on Sunday. The leader had a large following in other parts of the Philippines also.

We encountered others who held to a mixture of various beliefs – all combined into one. What confusion! These wonderful, loving, kind people were all sincere in what they believed from what they had been taught. But, they had missed the only true and living God -- Father, Son, and Holy Spirit. They were blinded to the truth or chose to believe untruth. How crucial it is that those of us who know the truth, as revealed by the Holy Spirit, reach out to those still in darkness.

It is crucial that we continue to get God's Word out to our world.

Leaders must be alert to which spirit is at work in their congregation. Sometimes an individual with a controlling, prideful, or critical spirit will seek to influence others in a fellowship of believers. They may even claim to have a "word" from the Lord, but it is manipulative or condemning. This is contrary to Scripture and must be discerned and dealt with quickly. Other times a person with a "religious" or "legalistic" spirit will be influencing others in leadership or some other area of ministry. This too must be addressed or it will infect others in a church and the grace of God will not continue to be evident.

In ministry, it is crucial to know what is happening in every situation. The *"discerning of spirits"* gift is not the same as natural discernment or use of common sense. On the outside, everything may look good when a new person comes into a fellowship of believers and expresses a desire to join in ministry or be part of a ministry team. But, later it becomes evident that their spirit is not right. This can create tension and disunity quickly. Be alert and allow the Holy Spirit to reveal the true character of the person before allowing them to serve in a leadership capacity.

There exists a real danger when a person appears to be a servant and later when put into Eldership or another position of authority, they expose their self-serving agenda or desire to control. Often, it's not until a person is given some measure of authority that their true spirit is revealed and then must be dealt with by the other leaders. The Holy Spirit will help you avoid trouble if you allow Him. Sometimes we just need to give Him time to speak into our life and life situations.

The Manifestation of "Power Gifts"

Faith
(I Corinthians 12:9)

Every believer must have faith in Jesus Christ in order to be "born-again" by the Holy Spirit. This is the baptism *in* the Spirit by which we are redeemed and saved. With regards to the continued work of the Spirit in a person's life, there may be times when a special measure of faith in God is needed. I often think of when Jesus' disciples were struggling and said to Him, *"Increase our faith!"* (Luke 17:5). They needed more faith to fulfill the assignments before them. We do also. This gift involves an inner conviction that compels the person to act in obedience in the face of great challenge.

The <u>Spirit Filled Life Bible</u> reveals four aspects of the "gift of faith". They are as follows:

A. Supernatural ability to believe God without doubt.

B. Supernatural ability to combat unbelief.

C. Supernatural ability to meet adverse circumstances with trust in God's messages and words.

D. Inner conviction impelled by an urgent and higher calling.[7]

This sounds like high adventure. Well, it is! This is where the Lord may choose to test us or call us up to a greater measure of ministry.

In the Old Testament, there are examples such as Noah being called to build the ark; Abraham being called to offer his son Isaac; David being called to go against the giant Goliath; Daniel being called to keep praying with the result of being thrown in the lion's den; Gideon being called to take three hundred soldiers against many thousands of enemies; Esther being called to appear before the king and risk her life, and numerous other examples.

The New Testament also identifies those called by God to face great and difficult challenges in faith.

After serving in the Seattle area for a couple years as NW Area Director of CBN Ministries (The Christian Broadcasting Network & Operation Blessing), I then began serving a church in the suburbs of Seattle. It was during this ministry that I was invited to a meeting at a downtown church to learn about March for Jesus (MFJ).

MFJ was a movement that had started in England and was spreading to the United States and other countries. Several Seattle prayer intercessors had received a video to show local pastors and ministry leaders. As I watched the video and saw God's people marching on city streets, carrying Praise banners and singing songs to the glory of God, I began to cry. It moved my heart deeply.

Those gathered for the showing were asked to pray about being involved and even leading a MFJ in Seattle. I left with more information, but knew that this required someone much more capable than me. Several days later I received a call from one of the intercessors asking if I would meet with her and another person about this great opportunity to lift Jesus up publicly in Seattle.

When I met with them, it became clear that they felt I was to lead this movement. I was surprised, but after listening to more details, agreed to pray about this. During this time of prayer, the Holy Spirit spoke into my heart – "You are the one to lead, trust Jesus to provide and guide."

I saw evidence of the *"gift of faith"* in action. When I accepted this great assignment, that only Jesus could do and complete, the Holy Spirit began flooding my mind with ideas of how God's people were to praise Him and make

Him known through the Seattle MFJ. The Spirit brought a great team together to serve on the Executive Council and we went into action, trusting Jesus each step of the planning and implementation.

The first year of the Seattle MFJ (1992) we saw many churches join in and thousands of believers gather in the city to exalt Jesus with singing, shouts of joy, dancing, and prayer. It was challenging but glorious! This special assignment requiring the impartation of the *"gift of faith"* continued for a total of nine years, every two years holding the celebration in a different part of the city.

There were many amazing testimonies of God's work in people's lives, as well as a noticeable impact on the spiritual climate of Seattle during this time. I was just Jesus' servant, given an overwhelming assignment, one that was accomplished through the *"gift of faith"* and His almighty power!

Another situation where the *"gift of faith"* was imparted was during my YWAM Outreach, when our team was in Chang Mai, Thailand. We were going to the largest Buddhist Temple in the region that overlooked the central part of the city. As I was preparing to go, the Holy Spirit again spoke into my heart.

This assignment included taking my shofar and blowing it when He showed me. My first thought was – "I'll be arrested if I blow it in the temple!". But, in obedience to the call of God, I took the shofar along and submitted, allowing the *"gift of faith"* to be manifested in me.

After our team climbed the many steps of the temple with dragons carved on both sides, we reached the top where the temple was. I instructed the team to spread out and allow the Holy Spirit to lead them where they were to pray.

As Vivian, myself, and one other person from the team walked around, we came to a place where there was a full view of the city below. There were large bells hanging there, where the monks would say their prayers over the city at specific times and ring the bells. The Spirit said – "Here's the place, sound the trumpet of the LORD over the city, declaring God's authority and confusing the enemy!".

Receiving boldness from Him, I stood at the edge and sounded the trumpet with three loud blasts representing God the Father, the Son, and the Holy Spirit. At the conclusion of the last trumpet blast, the three of us cried out *"Glory"* (Psalm 29:9)!

The Spirit not only opened the way for this spiritual warfare assignment to occur, but He also shielded me and the others during this time. We don't know what is happening in the spiritual realm during times like this, but we can believe that Jesus is doing His work through His servants and the power of the Holy Spirit.

Gifts of Healing
(I Corinthians 12:9)

Another translation is *"gifts of healings"* (I Corinthians 12:9 NKJV). The NIV Study Bible notes, "The double plural may suggest different kinds of illnesses and the various ways God heals them." [8]

Through this specific gift, the healing may be instantaneous or gradual, but it is still the work of God. It must be established that God alone is the Healer, not the person through whom the gift is imparted. It is a serious matter when someone whom the Spirit works through takes the credit and glory, thus leading people astray. There is only One Source of healing power -- God!

The Spirit Filled Life Bible reveals three aspects involved with this gift. They are as follows:

A. Refers to supernatural healing without human aid.

B. May include divinely assisted application of human instrumentation and medical means of treatment.

C. Does not discount the use of God's creative gifts. [9]

I love to see how Jesus called His disciples to apply the delegated power and authority that He imparted to them. In Luke 10:1, we discover, *"Now after this the Lord appointed seventy others, and sent them in pairs ahead of Him to every city and place where He Himself was going to come."* Jesus gave them all specific instructions, including the command – *"and heal those in it who are sick, and say to them, 'The kingdom of God has come near to you.' "* (Luke 10:9). This is an exciting ministry.

As mentioned previously regarding the "fruit" of joy, when these disciples came back with incredible testimonies, the response of Jesus is noted in Luke 10:21:

"At that very time He rejoiced greatly in the Holy Spirit, and said, 'I praise You, O Father, Lord of heaven and earth, that You have hidden these things from the wise and intelligent and have revealed them to infants. Yes, Father, for this way was well-pleasing in Your sight.' "

Jesus was doing the will of the Father by sending these *"appointed"* ones out as His ambassadors. The Holy Spirit filled Jesus with joy at the work of God that was accomplished through these simple servants who went out and impacted lives for the kingdom of God. When God's servants are open to whatever ways He chooses to work to bring Him glory, amazing results occur.

I believe it is important to note in following Jesus through the four Gospels, that He healed many during His ministry, but there were times that He did not heal everyone. Some whom He healed knew about Him, others did not. This is clearly a work of God and we must act in obedience to the Holy Spirit and leave the results with Him.

In the book of Acts, which I recognize as – the "acts" of the Holy Spirit in and through the followers of Jesus – we have numerous instances where the Holy Spirit imparted the *"gifts of healing"* to individuals.

One of the first deacons, Philip, was called out to share Jesus as the Messiah in Samaria during a time of persecution in the early Church. Acts 8:5-8 (NIV) tells us:

"Philip went down to a city in Samaria and proclaimed Christ there. When the crowds heard Philip and saw the miraculous signs he did, they all paid close attention to what he said....and many paralytics and cripples were healed. So there was great joy in that city."

Acts 9:32-35 (NIV) records where the Apostle Peter was called upon by the Holy Spirit to exercise the *"gifts of healing"*:

"As Peter traveled about the country, he went to visit the saints in Lydda. There he found a man named Aeneas, a paralytic who had been bedridden for eight years. 'Aeneas,' Peter said to him, 'Jesus Christ heals you. Get up and take care of your mat.' Immediately Aeneas got up. All those who lived in Lydda and Sharon saw him and turned to the Lord."

The Apostle Paul also experienced this work of the Holy Spirit in his ministry. Acts 14:8-10 (NIV) reveals:

"In Lystra there sat a man crippled in his feet, who was lame from birth and had never walked.

He listened to Paul as he was speaking. Paul looked directly at him, saw that he had faith to be healed and called out, 'Stand up on your feet!' At that, the man jumped up and began to walk."

The acts of the Holy Spirit involve divine healing. When the Holy Spirit is doing the work, people pay attention and it provides an opportunity to declare Jesus and His kingdom.

We will continually encounter people in need of healing. There is always a place to pray for the sick, but we should be yielded and open to the Holy Spirit when He imparts the *"gifts of healing"* and calls us to be obedient in declaring God's power.

Before our YWAM team arrived in the Philippines, our CDTS Outreach leader shared about a previous YWAM team that had sensed Jesus calling them to go to a local hospital and pray for each person there. They were granted permission to do this and those on the team spread out and went to each bed praying as the Holy Spirit led them.

A week later, this team returned to do the same thing and the hospital director met them and told them there was no need because all the sick people had been healed and had gone home! The Holy Spirit chose to impart the *"gifts of healing"* to each team member on that prior visit and there were incredible results. It is His work.

Our YWAM team reached out to many people in the Philippines where the Lord appointed us for a month. On the last night, before we were to leave, our team held a mini-crusade on the front porch of the house we stayed in.

Many children, youth, and adults came to see what it was about, after all, our team provided lots of good entertainment for their normally simple lives. At the end of the presentation, people were invited to come inside the house for refreshments and a time of prayer. As we were together, one of our team members felt a strong urge to pray for a girl of the village who was deaf. She was in the room, so I invited the team member to go ahead and pray for her.

There was no miraculous healing that night, but as a team, we were open to whatever the Holy Spirit wanted to do. The team member who was prompted by the Holy Spirit was obedient to pray for the deaf girl and trust Him for the results. The healing may have happened later, either instantaneously or at the hands of a physician. We don't know what happened after we left, that's God's part.

It is a delight to be Jesus' ambassador and bring joy to His heart through the work of the Spirit.

Effecting of Miracles
(I Corinthians 12:10)

This impartation is also referred to as, *"working of miracles"* (I Corinthians 12:10 NKJV). This gift is the Spirit-given ability to do supernatural, unexplainable acts for the glory of God.

The <u>Spirit Filled Life Bible</u> notes the following aspects of this gift:

A. Supernatural power to intervene and counteract earthly and evil forces.

B. Literally means a display of power giving the ability to go beyond the natural.

C. Operates closely with the gift of faith and healings to bring authority over sin, Satan, sickness and the binding forces of this age.[10]

Jesus provides numerous examples of His miraculous power, such as, calming the storm on the lake (Matthew 8:26); raising the dead girl to life (Matthew 9:25); walking on the water to meet his disciples (Matthew 14:25); the demonic deliverance of two men living in the region of the Gadarenes (Matthew 8:32-33), the feeding of the five thousand (Matthews 14:19-21), and many others.

Matthew 10:1 tells us what Jesus initiated,

"Jesus summoned His twelve disciples, and gave them authority over unclean spirits, to cast them out, and to heal every kind of disease and sickness."

Again, we see Jesus imparting God's power to common individuals to do His work on the earth. These were not educated, trained men. They were in continual training as they followed and obeyed Jesus. As Jesus' disciples we must do the same.

After the Pentecost revival when about 3,000 were baptized in one day, we hear about the continued convergence of the Spirit among them with miracles.

Acts 2:43 (NIV) records that, *"Everyone was filled with awe, and many wonders and miraculous signs were done by the apostles."* Glory to God!

Philip was not only called to exercise the *"gifts of healing"*, but also *"miraculous signs"*. Those in Samaria *"...heard and saw the signs which he was performing."* (Acts 8:6). It was evident that the power of God was at work through Philip, as revealed in Acts 8:7 (NIV) – *"With shrieks, evil spirits came out of many..."*.

In Acts 9:36-41 we see that the Holy Spirit called the Apostle Peter to pray over Tabitha (also known as Dorcas) who had died. She was raised back to life miraculously!

The Apostle Paul was used in a very unusual manner in Ephesus:

"And God was performing extraordinary miracles by the hands of Paul, so that handkerchiefs or aprons were even carried from his body to the sick, and the diseases left them and the evil spirits went out." (Acts 19:11-12)

How strange that God would use pieces of cloth passed from Paul to the sick to work miracles. This is a mystery, but obviously a "God-thing". As we go forth in ministry and missions serving Jesus, there may be situations where He desires to do miracles through the Holy Spirit.

It may be for basic provision of food, when nothing more is available. It may be when a catastrophic storm is threatening and your life is in danger. It may be that a demon-possessed person is seeking to hinder ministry and needs to be delivered. It may be that someone has just died and God wants to raise them back to life. The Lord continues to accomplish these miracles in our time and uses faithful believers in His work.

Again, we must never forget that this is God's work. As the beautiful old hymn states – "God moves in a mysterious way, His wonders to perform." Don't ever underestimate the power of God and the manner in which He may choose to demonstrate that power through the *"effecting of miracles"*.

Always be sure to give God the glory when miracles do happen.

The Manifestation of "Exhortation Gifts"

<u>Prophecy</u>
(I Corinthians 12:10)

This gift involves a Spirit-inspired utterance in a "known" or native language. It is spontaneous and comes from the

Holy Spirit, not from someone's forethought. The prophecy given must agree with Scripture as a whole and should edify, exhort, comfort, or build up the hearers. The prophecy that is spoken should be judged or discerned by a leader or leaders who are present.

Not every prophecy spoken is for everyone hearing the words, although at times it may be for the whole group. The prophecy may also be given to an individual who then writes it down and submits it to leadership for approval to be shared.

This specific gift of the Spirit is different from the motivational gift of "prophesying" revealed in Romans 12:6. Please refer back to the definition of that gift under the "Motivational Gifts" section in the previous chapter.

The Spirit Filled Life Bible provides five aspects of this gift and its use. They are as follows:

A. Divinely inspired and anointed utterance.

B. Supernatural proclamation in a known language.

C. Manifestation of the Spirit of God – not of intellect (I Corinthians 12:7).

D. May be possessed and operated by all who have the infilling of the Holy Spirit (I Corinthians 14:31).

E. Intellect, faith, and will are operative in this gift, but its exercise is not intellectually based. It is calling forth words from the Spirit of God.[11]

An example of the application of this gift is found in Acts 11:27-28. Take note of what transpires in this situation:

"Now at this time some prophets came down from Jerusalem to Antioch. One of them named Agabus stood up and began to indicate by the Spirit that there would certainly be a great famine all over the world. And this took place in the reign of Claudius."

Agabus was used of the Holy Spirit to predict and prepare God's people for what was soon to take place. It was God's grace being revealed through this spoken prophecy.

Another occurrence of this gift being imparted is found in Acts 13:2-3, we are told:

"While they were ministering to the Lord and fasting, the Holy Spirit said, 'Set apart for Me Barnabas and Saul for the work to which I have called them.' Then, when they had fasted and prayed and laid their hands on them, they sent them away."

The NIV Study Bible notes – "Paul's first missionary journey did not result from a planning session but from the Spirit's initiative as the leaders worshipped. The communication from the Holy Spirit may have come through the prophets." [12]

It is evident that the Spirit was working and it was His initiative that this special assignment was given to Barnabas and Saul (later known as Paul). The Holy Spirit may have spoken through one of the prophets or teachers (Acts 13:1), or through any other Spirit-filled believer present. He chooses "whom" He will use to reveal His message to be acted upon.

Acts 13:4 reveals further acknowledgement of the Spirit's convergence. We are told -- *"So, being sent out by the Holy Spirit, they went down to..."*.

As Jesus calls certain believers to go out on specific kingdom assignments, He will confirm the call through the Holy Spirit and others.

It is unwise for a person to go out in ministry without a spiritual covering and confirmation. It is always God's will to be *"sent out by the Holy Spirit"* with the endorsement of other mature believers.

Scripture reveals another situation that most likely involved the gift of prophecy. In Acts 21:4 (NIV) we read of the encounter that Paul had after he landed in Tyre on a missionary voyage:

"Finding the disciples there, we stayed with them seven days. Through the Spirit they urged Paul

not to go on to Jerusalem."

Then, shortly after this the Apostle Paul encounters others who the Spirit used with this specific gift at the next stop in his voyage. In Acts 21:8-9 (NIV) we read that:

"Leaving the next day, we reached Caesarea and stayed at the house of Philip the evangelist, one of the Seven. He had four unmarried daughters who prophesied."

It appears that the Holy Spirit had imparted to these women the ability to prophesy and bring forth God's specific revelation to others on a regular basis.

While staying with Philip a prophecy came forth:

"As we were staying there for some days, a certain prophet named Agabus came down from Judea. And coming to us, he took Paul's belt and bound his own feet and hands, and said, 'This is what the Holy Spirit says: In this way the Jews at Jerusalem will bind the man who owns this belt and deliver him into the hands of the Gentiles.' " (Acts 21:10-11)

We know his prophecy was valid because this is exactly what happened to the Apostle Paul when he arrived in Jerusalem. Take special note that Agabus states, *"This is what the Holy Spirit says..."*. This is an important part of operating in the gift of prophecy, it is God's revelation and not of human origin.

Some question whether this type of prophecy is still happening today. They confuse this supernatural gift of the Spirit with the inspiration that the Holy Spirit gave in writing the Scriptures. They are separate and distinct, although both originate with the Holy Spirit. No one is to add to God's holy and inspired Word, which we know as the Bible.

But, neither can we limit the Holy Spirit's continued work in setting apart individuals for ministry, revealing future matters in a person's life or warning of critical events yet to happen. The Holy Spirit is God and still chooses to intervene in the affairs of mankind to guide Christ-followers.

In my own life there have been those whom the Spirit has used to encourage me through the gift of prophecy. During the Teaching Phase of my CDTS in Kona, Hawaii, a YWAM leader named Peter Helms from Holland spoke to our class. Time was set aside for him to prophesy over the students. I am thankful that someone was recording each one. I still have the printed copy of the prophetic word spoken by Peter (see Appendix A).

After the CDTS teams returned from Outreach in Thailand and the Philippines a Celebration Banquet was held. At the conclusion of the meal and the sharing of testimonies, our leaders, Howard and Sue Bruce, invited students to come up for prayer.

When Vivian and I came up, Howard was given a

prophecy for me through the Holy Spirit. It was not recorded, but the words I distinctly remember were: "In the past you had to take from the bottom, but in the days ahead the Lord is going to allow you to take from the top. The Lord is showing me a picture of you reaching up to the top."

Upon returning to Seattle after the CDTS experience, the Lord called Vivian and I to pray for a church to serve. I had been serving in the International Church of the Foursquare Gospel prior to going on the CDTS and I continued to affiliate with this denomination. I fully expected the Lord to open up a church to serve in this fellowship. There were no church openings at the time, so I sought out other employment to provide for our needs.

One day I received a call asking if I would preach at a church in North Bend, Washington. I accepted and discovered that the church was affiliated with the Baptist General Conference (now Converge Worldwide). The church had been without a pastor for over six months and 48 pastors had applied for the position, but the leadership did not feel any of these were to serve the church.

On the Sunday that I was to preach, Vivian and I arrived at this 104 year old church and as I began walking up the steps, the Holy Spirit clearly said, "This is where you are going to serve Jesus". I paused for a moment and said to myself, "I'll preach here, but I won't be serving a Baptist church." After the message, Vivian and I stayed to enjoy a time fellowship with the congregation, especially since they were serving fresh strawberries over ice cream!

On the way out the door, the chairman of the church Board came up and said, "Pete, I've talked to several other Board members and we want to ask you to apply to be our pastor." I hesitated, but at his insistence, took the application. I later filled it out and sub-mitted it…the rest is history.

I've learned the Lord wants His servants to be "kingdom-minded" and not limit Him to denominations or churches. Vivian and I had the privilege of serving this wonderful congregation in the Snoqualmie Valley, thirty five miles east of Seattle, for over eleven years.

Serving there as pastor is part of what the Spirit was revealing earlier as "taking from the top".

Another aspect of "taking from the top" in ministry has been the privilege of teaching at different YWAM bases for their DTS. I have greatly enjoyed teaching on the topic of "The Ministry and Empowerment of the Holy Spirit". I see this as essential training for those being sent out in missions.

Many of the students and staff have grown up with little knowledge or understanding of the Spirit and how He is to be at work in their personal life and calling. It's my heart's desire to impart to others from God's Word and my experience how the Holy Spirit is working to fulfill the Great Commission of Christ.

The next kingdom assignment for me was to be the Lead Pastor at Lighthouse Christian Church in Warrenton, Oregon. This is another fulfillment of "taking from the top". There has been an incredible openness and responsiveness to the Lord's leading. The Elders and people truly desire to be led of the Holy Spirit and bring glory to God.

There have been times when I have been praying over an individual and the Holy Spirit will impart the gift of prophecy to me and I will simply speak forth what the Spirit is revealing for that person at that time.

This happened during one of the Lighthouse Christian Church "Praise & Prayer Gatherings", which we have twice a month on a Thursday evening. The Elders felt we should announce to the congregation on Sunday that at the next gathering, there would be a special time for anointing the sick and praying over them (James 5:14-15).

Many responded and came forward that night. As they came, I asked different Elders to anoint the person and offer a prayer in faith. After certain individuals were prayed for, the Holy Spirit gave me a prophecy for them. It was unplanned and spontaneous, but truly God-glorifying. At one point, I felt led to ask if there was anyone else present who had a revelation for an individual that was anointed with oil. Different people shared what the Holy Spirit was giving them for that person. We left that evening having experienced a wonderful work of God.

At the conclusion of each Sunday Worship, people are encouraged to come up if they desire to accept Christ or be prayed for in any way. On occasion, the Spirit will give me a prophecy for the person who has come up to be ministered to. I never know when this will happen but seek to be open for when it does. Other people are now available up front after the Worship to be used of the Spirit to minister as He directs them. It is truly edifying!

Dr. Doug Heck, a pastor that I served with many years in Seattle, goes regularly to China and South Korea. When he has shared the message the Lord has given him for the group he is meeting with, he ministers by giving a prophecy to certain individuals, allowing the Holy Spirit to speak directly into the lives of those who have come. It is a God-glorifying experience that gives strength to those who receive what the Lord reveals. These servants are blessed greatly as a result.

The Apostle Paul speaks to the validity and importance of this gift in I Corinthians 14:1-5. Take some time to read and reflect on his instruction.

Speaking in Various Kinds of Tongues

(I Corinthians 12:10)

This is clearly referring to *"speaking in tongues"* (I Corinthians 12:30; 13:8: 14:4-5).

There are those today who question whether speaking in tongues, as the early Church experienced, is still valid today. But for the millions of believers worldwide who do speak in tongues, it is not an issue. It's a reality.

For those who have not had this experience, it can be confusing and some choose to deny this work of the Holy Spirit. As I have stated before, from my experience in ministry, what people don't understand they are fearful of. This perspective limits what the Holy Spirit may desire to do in a person's life.

I recall distinctly my first exposure to speaking in tongues publicly. I started dating a girl from my high school who attended a different church than the one I grew up in. I was raised in the Christian Reformed Church denomination, which at that time taught that speaking in tongues ended with the original Apostles. When she invited me to attend an evening worship, I was in for a surprise. Not only was there a woman pastor, but speaking in tongues and dancing in the aisles! I was exposed to something that I didn't realize existed. But, there was joy in the worship and I was encouraged to see the freedom of expression that took place.

Several years later, while serving as a Student Minister in Shenandoah National Park, I became friends with a National Park Ranger. He told me about his experience with the Holy Spirit and speaking in tongues. That night, by myself in my cabin, I asked Jesus to allow me to speak in tongues if this was His will. Nothing happened.

It wasn't until a number of years later, while serving as Lead Pastor at Millgrove Christian Reformed Church near Allegan, Michigan, that I experienced a unique in-filling of the Spirit with speaking in tongues. I was experiencing a crisis in ministry and had asked another pastor in the area to come over and pray with Vivian and myself.

When this pastor came in the door, he said – "Pete, you need to be baptized with the Holy Spirit. Are you willing to give up everything to God and trust Him in this?" I realized that if I received this baptism with the Spirit, it would mean leaving the denomination that I was raised in, had been serving in, was receiving a good salary in, and was very comfortable in. There would be many "un-knowns" for me and my family, should I experience the speaking in tongues.

But, I wanted all that God had for me. I was willing to sacrifice whatever needed to be sacrificed in order to be in His will. When I affirmed to this fellow-pastor that I was willing, he put his hand on my head and began praying in tongues over me. While he was praying, I experienced God's Presence in a new, fresh way. And, I began speaking in tongues also. It seemed to flow very naturally, which was totally un-natural given my difficulty with speaking other languages.

While speaking in tongues, I experienced a great peace and joy simultaneously. I also was given a vision of someone in my congregation who was being miraculously healed at that very moment.

Two days later, I called this person to share what I knew and she was baffled at how I could have been aware of this. I came to find out that she also had an experience involving the baptism with the Spirit and had spoken in tongues for many years. Jesus was leading me in a fresh new way for His purpose and glory.

About six months after this impartation of the Holy Spirit, I knew the Lord was calling me to continue my education and pursue a Master's degree in ministry. He led me to Regent University in Virginia Beach, VA which meant a major move and faith for God's provision for our family.

While in school, I had the privilege of working with the guests on *The 700 Club* television program. I also got to know the people scheduling the program content each day. When there was a request for a Regent University student to share their personal experience about the "baptism with the Spirit" on an up-coming program, I volunteered. It was an exciting day when I appeared on national television to share how the Holy Spirit had brought about a change in my life. He works all things together for our good and His glory.

I believe it is important to understand that there is a "two-fold" function of speaking in *various kinds of tongues* (I Corinthians 12:10, 28). These are both Spirit initiated. However, one is for personal edification and the other is for public exhortation in the fellowship of believers. Let's examine both of these convergence experiences.

A. Tongues for Personal Edification

Let's look at a variety of Scriptures related to this aspect and come to an understanding of its use for the believer.

■ **I Corinthians 14:2, 4a**

"For one who speaks in a tongue does not speak to men but to God; for no one understands, him; but in his spirit he speaks mysteries...One who speaks in a tongue edifies himself..."

Here, the Apostle Paul is giving instruction on the use of Holy Spirit initiated tongues for private use. In this use of tongues, a person *"in his spirit he speaks mysteries"* or *"utters mysteries with his spirit"* (I Corinthians 14:2 NIV). This results in being personally edified in one's faith in God.

Some people refer to this experience as their "spiritual prayer language". It is mostly used privately in a devotional manner as they lift praise to God or intercede for themselves and others. They may on occasion utter a prayer in spiritual tongues as they pray with another person or in a prayer gathering. This is done in a quiet, caring manner.

■ **Romans 8:26-27**

"In the same way the Spirit also helps our weakness; for we do not know how to pray as we should, but the Spirit Himself intercedes for us with groaning too deep for words; and He who searches the hearts knows what the mind of the Spirit is, because He intercedes for the saints according to the will of God."

Here, the Apostle Paul is pointing out that when a believer encounters a situation where they cannot pray in their native language or are overwhelmed and unsure how to pray, that the Spirit enables them to pray in tongues.

This praying in the Spirit, or allowing the Spirit to manifest Himself through the believer in a heavenly language, accomplishes God's will. The person does not know what they are praying, but becomes a vessel whereby *"the Spirit Himself intercedes for us with groaning too deep for words"* (v. 26). The believer cannot express them in his or her native tongue, but the Spirit can through a heavenly tongue or spiritual prayer language.

In my own personal prayer life, I have found great peace in submitting myself to the Holy Spirit and praying in tongues over a situation or person. When I cannot utter or express my prayer in English, I allow the Holy Spirit to take over in my heavenly prayer language. I am comforted to know this prayer is received by the Father *"who searches the hearts and knows what the mind of the Spirit is"* (v. 27). We can be confident that God is working through the prayer uttered by the Spirit, which is a marvelous spiritual mystery.

■ **Ephesians 6:18**

"With all prayer and petition pray at all times in the Spirit..."

This is revealed in the context of spiritual warfare. The Apostle Paul knew firsthand what spiritual warfare was all about! In preparing the Christ-follower for doing spiritual battle, he concludes his instruction with the importance of praying *"in the Spirit"*. We need the Holy

Spirit's help in dealing with the powers of darkness that come against us.

We are instructed to *"pray in the Spirit on all occasions with all kinds of prayer..."* (v.18 NIV). This means that we should not limit the work of the Spirit in our lives. He desires for us to be open to His work in and through us on all occasions.

The phrase *"all kinds of prayer"* literally means, "every order of praying". The different manners of praying would include both praying with one's mind in our native language and praying in the Spirit with speaking in tongues.

Praying in the Spirit through tongues serves as an effective weapon of spiritual warfare to defeat the work of Satan and his demons. These evil forces certainly cannot understand the language of the Spirit, so we can use it for protection along with declaring the name of Jesus and the blood of Jesus (Revelation 12:11). In doing so, we are taking the offensive in spiritual warfare and acknowledging that the battle is the Lord's.

■ **I Corinthians 14:14-15**

"For if I pray in a tongue, my sprit prays, but my mind is unfruitful. What is the outcome then? I will pray with the spirit and I will pray with the mind also..."

231

The Apostle Paul makes a clear distinction between praying to God with our mind in our native tongue and praying to God with our spirit through the work of the Holy Spirit in our heavenly language. Both manners of praying are in order to God.

When we *"pray in a tongue"* the Holy Spirit moves upon our spirit and we do not know what we are specifically praying in our mind, except that it is God doing it. We can be assured it is having a power impact.

So then, why don't we only pray in tongues all the time? Because the Lord wants us to pray with our mind and also with our spirit as prompted by the Holy Spirit, when it is necessary. Certainly we should be led by the Spirit whenever we pray with our mind. We always want to follow His lead.

■ **Jude 20-21**

"But you, beloved, building yourselves up on your most holy faith, pray in the Holy Spirit, keep yourselves in the love of God, waiting anxiously for the mercy of our Lord Jesus Christ to eternal life".

Each day believers need to build themselves up in their *"most holy faith"*. This building up process means that we put forth effort to stay close to Jesus. This comes through reading Scripture, listening to Christian songs, using daily devotionals, being consistent in Spirit-led worship, being

232

involved in Bible study growth groups, and having fellowship with other believers all help us grow in the grace and knowledge of our Lord.

I've included some devotional writings from Anne Graham Lotz, daughter of Dr. Billy Graham, in Appendix C. These are examples of how the insight of others can build up our spirit. They have encouraged me greatly in my faith-growth process.

Another wonderful growth tool is the book, I Want To Know More Of Christ – A Daily Devotional On His Matchless Names, by Steve Hall. Steve is a special Brother in Christ with a passion to make Jesus known to everyone. You can order a book at www.KnowingMoreOfChrist.com.

Our world continually tries to pollute our minds and draw us away from the things of God. Sometimes it seems like we are being bomb-barded from every side.

Jude points out to us the importance of also *"praying in the Holy Spirit"* as part of our building up process. This is how we strengthen our relationship with God and persevere in our faith. This happens when we pray in both our native language and in our spiritual language of tongues.

The Holy Spirit is not only our Teacher, but our Helper and Counselor. He knows best what we need and the sooner we realize this, the more we will seek His leading through our praying. Allow the Spirit to prompt you as you come to "Abba" Father, and Jesus, in prayer each day.

■ **Revelation 1:10**

"I was in the Spirit on the Lord's day, and I heard behind me a loud voice...".

I personally believe that as the Apostle John was worshipping God that day while in exile, he was praying in the Spirit, through the speaking in tongues. As a worshipper who was *"in the Spirit"*, he was "under the complete influence of the Holy Spirit. Some would say that John was in 'a state of spiritual exaltation' ". [13]

There are times in my personal worship of the Lord, that I enter into a state of spiritual exaltation and I begin praising God in tongues. My joy is inexpressible and the Spirit allows me to worship the Lord in a glorifying manner. I celebrate this spiritual freedom in Christ.

In reality, our minds limit us in praying and praising God. But, worship from our spirit through the Holy Spirit is unlimited and uninhibited! John encountered the risen Christ in a very special and unique manner during this time so that His revelation might go forth to the world. As we worship the same risen Christ, may we hear His voice and be obedient to do what He says.

B. Tongues for Public Exhortation

In I Corinthians 14, the Apostle Paul gives very specific instructions on the place of tongues in public exhortation.

In order to avoid confusion or misunderstanding, it is important for the Pastor, an Elder, or a leader to give instructions. They should give an explanation about speaking in tongues publically for exhortation, so all know what is happening and that it is in accord with God's Word.

I've identified the following aspects that I believe are key matters revealed in this chapter of Scripture. They are:

- Public speaking in tongues for exhortation only edifies those worshipping when there is an interpretation that follows (v. 5).

- The person prompted by the Holy Spirit to speak in tongues for public exhortation should also pray for the interpretation (v. 13).

- If the person who spoke in tongues publically for exhortation does not receive an interpretation, the Holy Spirit may give the interpretation to another (v. 27) (see also I Corinthians 12:10).

- Speaking in tongues publically for exhortation should be done properly and in an orderly manner (v. 40).

- The speaking in tongues publically for exhortation is to be limited to sequences of two or three persons (v. 27).

- Speaking in tongues should not be forbidden for public exhortation (v. 39).

- Speaking in tongues publically for exhortation is to be for the strengthening and edification of the church (v. 5, 26).

- The gift of prophecy or prophesying is preferred over speaking in tongues for public exhortation, unless there is an interpretation (v. 1, 5).

Along with these instructions, it is important to know that the Spirit works only to edify the church, which means that what is spoken is not of a critical or condemning nature.

The pastor, elders, or leader present must discern how the Spirit is working. It is out of order for someone to interrupt a sermon, song, or another person praying, to speak in tongues publically for exhortation.

The one leading the time of corporate worship may allow a time of silence to wait on the Lord and allow the Spirit to bring forth a prophecy or speaking in tongues with interpretation.

It may be advisable to inform those gathered for worship that if they feel the Holy Spirit prompting them, they are to indicate such by writing a note and giving it to the pastor or an elder for discernment. If the leadership trusts the person requesting to be used of the Holy Spirit and believe it is appropriate timing, they may grant permission. This is not controlling the moving of the Spirit, but merely maintaining order within the fellowship of worshippers.

Depending on the situation, context, and leadership, it may be permissible to act upon the prompting of the Spirit without receiving permission first. Such was the case during a worship time at the CDTS that I was part of. Here is what took place.

During one particular time in worship involving our school of over a hundred students, I felt over-whelmed by the Presence of the Holy Spirit while singing a song. I felt prompted to speak in tongues publically for exhortation.

I was hesitant because nothing had been said to the students prior in over a month of daily meetings. But, I felt the Spirit moving upon me in an increasing measure, so that my heart was racing. I sensed Him saying – "Be obedient and trust me". I determined that if the Praise Team leader paused between songs longer than usual, that I was to speak out.

When the song ended and another song did not begin, I submitted and spoke out loud in tongues as the Spirit enabled me. When I stopped, our school leader came running down the center isle from the back of the room and said – "Wait, we must wait for an interpretation to this!" It was very silent throughout the room. I was not prompted by the Spirit to give the interpretation. We waited, until from the back of the room a female student spoke forth the interpretation in English. I don't remember the details of the interpretation, but I do know it was edifying to all those present and encouraged us in our trust in the Lord.

After our worship time, when we were dismissed, the school leader came up to me and said that it had been a long time since there had been a speaking in tongues with interpretation at a CDTS worship. He was excited and grateful for what the Spirit was doing in our midst.

Another experience of this nature took place over seven years later during a sabbatical I took while serving at North Bend Community Church. Vivian and I volunteered to be YWAM Mission Builders for part of this time away from the church. The Lord had led us to a YWAM base in Jamaica for five weeks to serve where we were most needed. We became very close to the director, staff, and the DTS students from various countries.

One evening during a time of corporate worship, I sensed the prompting of the Spirit to speak in tongues publically for exhortation. While the others continued in singing, I went up to the director sitting in the front row and shared with her what I was sensing. I submitted the matter to her for discernment and mentioned that I would explain what was to take place so there would be no confusion. I then returned to my seat several rows back.

After the next song was finished, the director went up to the front and asked everyone to sit down. She then asked me to come up and explain what the Holy Spirit wanted to do in our midst. I came up and gave a brief explanation, then said, "Let's just be still in the Lord's Presence and wait for the Spirit to speak."

I went back to my seat and when the Spirit prompted me, I stood up and spoke in tongues as the Spirit enabled me. When the speaking in tongues ended, I remained standing and waited. Soon the interpretation in English came forth and the Holy Spirit brought forth words of hope, faith, and encouragement to all gathered there.

The Holy Spirit desires to keep working in the lives of God's people. We never know what He may reveal to keep us looking to Jesus and fulfilling His plan for our lives. What a blessing it is when He breaks through to touch our hearts and change our lives through the gifts He imparts.

Jack Hayford has written an excellent book entitled, The Beauty Of Spiritual Language – My Journey Toward the Heart of God, which tells his own experience and helps people understand how God is still working through the speaking in tongues. If you have more questions about the blessing of speaking or singing in tongues by the Spirit, I'd advise you to get this book and increase your understanding further. It's important to learn from each other in ministry.

Interpretation of Tongues
(I Corinthians 12:10)

Interpretation is necessary with regard to speaking in tongues as a public exhortation. The Apostle Paul is very clear in explaining this in I Corinthians 14:6-13. He concludes his instruction saying, *"Therefore let one who speaks in a tongue pray that he may interpret."* (v. 13).

Looking back to I Corinthians 12:10, the revelation

given here points to *"...another the interpretation of tongues.".*

Therefore, even though it is preferable that the person speaking in tongues also interpret, it is not always the case. It may be that the Spirit will use *"another"* to declare the message to be given in the native language of those present.

I Corinthians 14:27 points out to us, *"If anyone speaks in a tongue...one must interpret."* This reveals that whether the interpreter is the one who spoke *"in a tongue"* or another person present, the key point is that the speaking in tongues for public edification is to be followed by an interpretation.

You might be asking – "If someone speaks in tongues publicly, but does not give an interpretation, how will I know if the Spirit is prompting me to deliver it?"

The Holy Spirit works in us individually and in His own special way. I believe He will let you know. For myself, I know the special prompting. My heart starts racing and I feel an overwhelming Presence of the Lord on me.

Another question you might be asking is – "Will I know what the interpretation is or what words to say before I speak?" Not usually, but the Spirit may put one or two words in your mind initially. He then wants you to continue allowing Him to speak the message as He enables you. It is wonderful to just let Him give you the words to speak out – words of edification.

This truly involves having faith in Jesus and what He wants to do through the Spirit in the midst of His people.

We are simply obedient vessels He chooses to speak through.

Some have asked me, "Pete, how will I know if the interpretation is correct when someone speaks it?" This is very important. When an interpretation is given it will not contradict Scripture, and as already mentioned, it will not be condemning or criticizing. The message will be edifying, for the common good, imparting hope, faith, and encouragement.

Remember, the foundation and motivation for the operation of all spiritual gifts is LOVE.

Someone once said that the spiritual gifts revealed in I Corinthians 12 & 14 are like the bread of a sandwich, and I Corinthians 13 is the meat inside. We need the meat to make God's will complete, right?

We learn as we allow God to work. It may be a bit uncomfortable or awkward initially, but don't let that stop you from being used of the Lord. We grow by stepping out in faith and obedience. Over time, you may feel a greater freedom to accept the Spirit's prompting and operate in these manifestation gifts. Operating in these gifts in a small group setting is often strengthening and affirming.

I recall while a student at Regent University, one of my professors asked us to gather in small circles of five to six students. He then said, "I want each of you to be still and wait on the Holy Spirit. When He shows you something, whatever it is, share it with your group."

After a period of silence, it was amazing what the Holy Spirit began to reveal to different ones in various groups.

He wanted the opportunity to reveal some matters of importance to the students in our class. I am so thankful that our professor was willing to allow this to happen. It encouraged me to be more open to the Spirit, as well as allowing Him to use others to minister to me.

I often think of Psalm 27:14 in this regards –

"Wait for the Lord;
Be strong and let your heart take courage;
Yes, wait for the Lord."

Leaders should be encouraged to allow for *"wait"* times in the groups they are called to lead. They might be surprised how the Spirit will encourage and help those present to *"take courage"* in the midst of life's challenges. When the Spirit of God is at work and we cooperate, He imparts spiritual strength. Let God use the *"wait"* factor in your relationship with Him.

God Loves Teamwork

In examining I Corinthians 12:4-31, Dr. John Maxwell focuses on the importance of seeing these gifts function in light of "team building". We are on God's team in kingdom ministry. With regard to using our gift in ministry, missions, or church teams we must keep the following matters in mind. Maxwell shares these insights:

1. The team possesses a variety of gifts or positions, but pursues the same goal and God (vv. 4-6).

2. Everyone has a contribution to make which benefits the team (v. 7).

3. God is the source of each gift, so He deserves the glory (vv. 8-10).

4. God chooses who has what gift, so we must not compete or compare (v. 11).

5. Team members are to function like the organs and muscles in a body (vv. 12-14).

6. No team member is less important than another; all are necessary (vv. 15-21).

7. Sometimes, the players who seem less important are actually more important (vv. 22-24).

8. God's goal is team harmony and mutual care (vv. 25, 26).

9. Although members are equally important, they are meant to be diverse (vv. 27, 28).

10. We should not compete with each other, but complete each other (vv. 29-31). [14]

Team leaders need to especially apply the insight given by Maxwell in overseeing the team and seeking to establish unity of purpose. This is crucial for attaining goals in the midst of the diversity of individuals with their different functions.

Francis Chan states, "If we are going to rediscover the power and presence of the Holy Spirit, we will need to begin listening to His voice and following His leading – not in the ways we think He should speak and lead, but in whatever He may call us to do." [15]

I wholeheartedly agree. God's Spirit is drawing us out to move out to reach out wherever He has placed us.

Each category of gifts – Ministry Gifts, Motivational Gifts, and Manifestation Gifts are significant from God's perspective and should be used without reservation to honor Him and impact others positively.

Chapter 10 – The Unique Filling of the Holy Spirit

Scripture reveals two outstanding spiritual experiences involving the Holy Spirit. One is essential for salvation, and the other is beneficial in ministry, personal edification, and worship. Both involve convergence with the work of the Spirit in a person's spirit. Both are a blessing from Jesus!

A. The Baptism *in* the Holy Spirit – the born-again conversion experience.

This is the initial conversion experience brought about by Jesus through the Holy Spirit when a person comes to faith in Christ.

After Jesus accomplished His work of salvation by dying on the cross and rising from the dead, He appeared to His disciples. In John 20:21-22, we see what happens when they encounter Him alive:

> *"So Jesus said to them again, 'Peace be with you; as the Father has sent Me, I also send you.' And when He had said this, He breathed on them and said to them, 'Receive the Holy Spirit.' "*

The resurrection of Jesus Christ, the Son of God, was the turning point of all history!

His work was complete. Salvation through Him was now available to all who would believe in Him.

The Apostle Paul tells us that if Jesus had not been raised to life again, then we would all remain in our sin. Which means, if He had died on the cross, but then remained in the grave, our sins would not be atoned for. Therefore, it was only after He arose that faith in Him would result in salvation or being "born-again". Listen to Paul's explanation in I Corinthians 15:17, 19:

"and if Christ has not been raised, your faith is worthless; you are still in your sins...If we have hoped in Christ in this life only, we are of all men most to be pitied."

The Spirit Filled Life Bible makes an interesting observation regarding this action of Jesus when He first appeared to His disciples. It tells us regarding John 20:22 – "The allusion to Genesis 2:7 is unmistakable. Now Jesus breathed life into His own. Some interpret the statement *"Receive the Holy Spirit"* as symbolic and as anticipating Pentecost. Others understand the Greek to denote immediacy in the sense of 'receive right now,' and view the day of the Lord's resurrection as marking the transition from the terms of the Old Covenant to those of the New Covenant. The old creation began with the breath of God;

now the new creation begins with the breath of God the Son." [1]

I hold to the latter view which is the literal revelation. This marks the conversion of these men who were trained up to be Jesus' disciples. Truly, they had faith prior, as Peter earlier declared – *"You are the Christ."* (Mark 8:29 NIV). But, it was a faith under the Old Covenant because complete salvation wasn't possible until after Christ's resurrection.

Jesus had clearly proclaimed to His disciples – *"The Spirit gives life; the flesh counts for nothing. The words I have spoken to you are spirit and they are life."* (John 6:63 NIV).

A powerful Spirit-dynamic happened that moment Jesus *"breathed on them and said to them, 'Receive the Holy Spirit."* (John 20:22). They were never the same from that point on! The Pentecost experience only added to their new life in the risen Jesus.

We know of others who saw Jesus alive after His Resurrection during the forty day period before He ascended back to heaven. There were the various women mentioned in the Gospels, as well as the eleven disciples. The Apostle Paul mentions in I Corinthians 15:6, that Jesus appeared to *"more than five hundred brethren at one time..."*, proving He was alive. Then there were those who accompanied Jesus to the place where He ascended. There was also the Apostle Paul (formerly Saul) who encountered the risen Jesus and was dramatically changed.

After Jesus' ascension and prior to Pentecost, which was ten days later, we discover a significant group of "believers" who were gathered together in prayer in Jerusalem. Acts 1:13-14, reveals the eleven disciples along with certain women and Mary the mother of Jesus, and his brothers were there.

Then, verse 15 tells us – *"At this time Peter stood up in the midst of the brethren (a gathering of about one hundred and twenty persons was there together)…"*. The NIV says these were "believers", where as the NKJV identifies them as "disciples". The terms are synonymous, and it is obvious that all one hundred and twenty were Christ-followers who were born-again previously by the Holy Spirit.

These individuals who gathered in prayer out of obedience to Jesus' command were clearly "believers" before Pentecost.

Jesus had foretold of being baptized "in" the Holy Spirit when He spoke in John 7:37-38. This Scripture tells us:

"Now on the last day, the great day of the feast, Jesus stood and cried out, saying, 'If anyone is thirsty, let him come to Me and drink. He who believes in Me, as the Scripture said, 'From his innermost being will flow rivers of living water.' "

The Apostle John clarifies what Jesus was referring to in verse 39 when he says:

"But this He spoke of the Spirit, whom those who believed in Him were to receive; for the Spirit was not yet given, because Jesus was not yet glorified." (John 7:39)

Jesus was *glorified in His* resurrection. He had a glorified, physical body, which made it possible for Him to appear and disappear as He chose.

After His resurrection, when He *"breathed"* on the original disciples, the Holy Spirit came into them and *"rivers of living water"* began flowing out of them as a result. This is truly glorious.

The Spirit Filled Life Bible comments on this significant passage with this explanation – "John interprets the words of Jesus to refer to the pouring out of the Holy Spirit that was still to come. The Holy Spirit existed from all eternity, but was not yet present in the sense indicated. Soon the fullness of the Spirit would be a blessing that all of God's people could experience." [2]

The Apostle Peter also refers to this in regards to the initial salvation experience when he states in Acts 2:38-39:

"And Peter said to them, 'Repent, and each of you be baptized in the name of Jesus Christ for the forgiveness of sins; and you shall receive the gift of the Holy Spirit. For the promise is for you

and your children and for all who are far off, as many as the Lord our God will call to Himself'."

He is revealing that the gift *of* the Holy Spirit or baptism *in* the Holy Spirit, which are the same, is available for salvation to those who were still unbelievers and not saved, if they would repent and confess Jesus. As we shall soon see, baptism *with* the Holy Spirit is available after being baptized *in* the Holy Spirit. Note the difference.

The *"promise"* that Peter mentions in verse 39 is in the context of salvation. I see the connection between this and the promise Peter earlier declared from the prophecy of Joel found in Acts 2:21 – *"AND IT SHALL BE THAT EVERYONE WHO CALLS ON THE NAME OF THE LORD WILL BE SAVED."*

This is the eternal promise of salvation given then and still given today to us, our children and *"...as many as the Lord our God shall call to Himself."*

It is obvious from Scripture that there were many who came to true saving faith in the risen Jesus prior to the manifestation of the Holy Spirit on the Day of Pentecost. These believers had experienced the baptism *in* the Holy Spirit unto conversion. This baptism makes the eternal difference in a person.

One becomes a child of God and is now led by the Spirit (Romans 8:14, 16). This baptism moves the believer from the kingdom of darkness to the kingdom of Light in Christ. As the Apostle Paul declares – we are *"Light in the Lord"* (Ephesians 5:8).

B. The Baptism *with* the Holy Spirit

The key question to ask is, "Who is the One that baptizes *with* the Holy Spirit?" John the Baptizer gives us the answer:

"As for me, I baptize you with water for repentance, but He who is coming after me is mightier than I, and I am not fit to remove His sandals; He will baptize you <u>with</u> the Holy Spirit and fire." (Matthew 3:11)

Then the Apostle John shares the testimony of John the Baptizer again in John 1:32-34 (NIV):

"Then John gave this testimony: 'I saw the Spirit come down from heaven as a dove and remain on him. I would not have known him, except the one who sent me to baptize with water told me 'The man on whom you see the Spirit come down and remain is he who will baptize <u>with</u> the Holy Spirit.' I have seen and I testify that this is the Son of God."

When did Jesus baptize *with* the Holy Spirit? Scripture reveals that this unique experience, beyond conversion, took place on the Day of Pentecost. Acts 2:4 tells us:

"And they were all filled <u>with</u> the Holy Spirit and began to speak with other tongues, as the Spirit was giving them utterance."

Jesus had to first ascend back to Heaven before He would baptize *"with the Spirit and fire"* (Matthew 3:11). He explains this to His followers after His resurrection and before His ascension so they know what to expect. Jesus says to them:

"And behold, I am sending forth the promise of My Father upon you; but you are to stay in the city until you are clothed <u>with</u> power from on high." (Luke 24:49)

This being *"clothed with"* is the same as being *"baptized with"*. It is an immersion or covering over with the power of God.

Also in Acts 1:4-5 we read of this revelation of Jesus:

"Gathering them together, He commanded them not to leave Jerusalem, but to wait for what the Father had promised, 'Which,' He said, 'you heard from Me; for John baptized you with water, but you shall be baptized <u>with</u> the Holy Spirit not many days from now' ".

Jesus confirms the sequence of this unique anointing of the Spirit upon His followers, those who would truly believe in Him after His resurrection.

Luke continues to inform us of what Jesus revealed about this baptism *with* the Holy Spirit in Acts 1:8 where we read:

"but you shall receive power when the Holy Spirit has come upon you; and you shall be My witnesses..."

The experience of being *"clothed <u>with</u> power from on high"* or being *"baptized <u>with</u> the Holy Spirit"* or *"power when the Holy Spirit <u>comes on you</u>"*, are all the same experience. This is Jesus' work through the Spirit given to those who already were baptized "in" the Spirit for conversion.

On the Day of Pentecost, the Apostle Peter refers to the words of the prophet Joel. This was to inform the crowd that gathered in Jerusalem of what was happening. When the Spirit manifested as He did, Peter declared:

"but this is what was spoken of through the prophet Joel:
'AND IT SHALL BE IN THE LAST
DAYS,' God says,
'THAT I WILL POUR FORTH OF MY
SPIRIT ON ALL MANKIND;
AND YOUR SONS AND YOUR

DAUGHTERS SHALL PROPHESY,
AND YOUR YOUNG MEN SHALL
SEE VISIONS,
AND YOUR OLD MEN SHALL
DREAM DREAMS;
EVEN ON MY BONDSLAVES,
BOTH MEN AND WOMEN,
I WILL IN THOSE DAYS POUR
FORTH OF MY SPIRIT
AND THEY SHALL PROPHESY.' "

(Acts 2:16-18)

The prophecy given hundreds of years prior was fulfilled that day. But wait, this anointing or empowering of the Spirit is not just about Jesus as the One who baptizes. Jesus Himself revealed that this is *"the promise of My Father"* (Luke 24:49) or *"the gift my Father promised"* (Acts 1:4 NIV)

Our Heavenly Father, desires to bestow this special *"gift"* upon those who belong to His Son. This *"gift"* or *"promise"* is power from on high. Power to be all Jesus has called us to be, to witness to the world about Who He is (Acts 1:8), as well as, praise Him in worship gloriously.

We know that the Father only gives good gifts, He is the Giver and we are the recipients. He knows that we need an on-going convergence experience of the Holy Spirit beyond the initial convergence experience of salvation.

We must be baptized *in* the Spirit to be born-again, but the Father offers us more – it is His *gift*, that we might live empowered lives through the Holy Spirit. Jesus refers to this very *gift* of the Father in Luke 11:13 (NIV):

"If you then, though you are evil, know how to give good gifts to your children, how much more will your Father in heaven give the Holy Spirit to those who ask him!"

For the early believers that experienced the baptism *with* the Spirit on the Day of Pentecost, it was necessary to continually seek the Holy Spirit's power and enabling to follow Jesus. This was evident when a crisis occurred in the Jerusalem church and we discover the following in Acts 4:31:

"And when they had prayed, the place where they had gathered together was shaken, and they were all filled <u>with</u> the Holy Spirit, and began to speak the word of God with boldness."

God's word clearly reveals God's manner of working in the lives of believers. This work or *"gift"* of the Father should cause us to seek Him more and yield to Him completely. For those who have experienced this baptism *with* the Spirit, it is crucial to continue in this "in-filling".

Jesus wants us to be built up in our faith and be bold in our witness. A believer can seek the baptism *with* the Spirit

255

at anytime and anywhere. In Scripture we find instances when leaders laid hands on people and the *"gift"* of the Father was bestowed on them. Others received it when they heard the revelation of God's truth and opened their heart to God's work in them.

The Apostle Paul gives instruction to believers in Ephesians 5:17-18:

"So then do not be foolish, but understand what the will of the Lord is. And do not get drunk with wine, for that is dissipation, but be filled <u>with</u> the Spirit."

It is God's will that we be under the continual influence of the Spirit, not the flesh.

The NIV Study Bible notes: "The Greek present tense is used to indicate that the filling of the Spirit is not a once-for-all experience. Repeatedly, as the occasion requires, the Spirit empowers for worship, service and testimony." [3]

The Spirit Filled Life Bible points out that, "The tense of the Greek for *be filled* makes clear that such a Spirit-filled condition does not stop with a single experience, but is maintained by 'continually being filled' as commanded here". [4]

This "filling" results in the outward actions of – *"speaking to one another in psalms and hymns and spiritual songs, singing and making melody with your heart to the Lord;"* (Ephesians 5:19). This is the expression of Spirit-filled worship. There is glorious praise!

I believe that for this impartation of the Spirit, it is necessary to first repent of known sins and renounce past involvement with the evil spirit world. Being cleansed of sin by the blood of Jesus is crucial to being completely open to the fullness of the Spirit.

As David prayed in Psalm 139:23-24 (NIV), so should someone seeking the infilling of the Holy Spirit for empowerment. David sought the Lord and prayed:

"Search me, O God, and know my heart; test me and know my anxious thoughts. See if there is any offensive way in me, and lead me in the way everlasting."

Our un-confessed sin is offensive to God and may block the work of the Spirit in our lives.

A suggested personal prayer of confession to use is:

"Dear Heavenly Father, forgive me where I have been involved in anything contrary to Your Word. I renounce my past involvement with (name specific matters). I put all these things under the blood of Jesus Christ, my Savior and Lord, casting them out now, never to return again. Lord, I ask that you fill those empty spaces with Your truth. I desire to be completely yielded to the Holy Spirit. In Jesus' Name I pray this. Amen." [5]

Now, if you desire to receive the *"gift of the Father"*, ask Jesus, the Baptizer in the Spirit, to clothe you with power from on high. This is a suggested prayer:

"Lord Jesus, as your child and faithful follower, I ask You to baptize me with the Holy Spirit for Your glory and give me a new Spirit-enabled language to use in prayer, praise, and the work of Your kingdom. I yield myself completely to You. Amen."

Begin praising Jesus and Abba, Father. Open your mouth and allow the utterance to come forth from your spirit, by the Holy Spirit.

It may seem awkward at first, that's OK. It may sound unintelligible, that's OK. On the day of Pentecost, those speaking in tongues were accused of being drunk (Acts 2:13, 15) because the sounds that came forth weren't intelligible. Don't be hindered by what you can't completely understand right now. Let go of any past inhibitions and let God do His wonderful work in you. More inspiration will come later as you seek the Lord on this.

I've heard of those who prayed for the baptism *with* the Spirit and it was at a different time, either alone or with others in worship, when they experienced a release in their spirit and began to speak in an unlearned, heavenly, spiritual prayer language. I refer to this personally as the "release of God" when it happens.

One instance I heard about was when a person suddenly began speaking in tongues for the first time while they were in the shower! Maybe they were singing praises and the Holy Spirit took over.

Don't limit Jesus, the Baptizer in the Spirit – just give Him the glory He is due and trust Him for what He wants to do in you.

New Testament Testimonies

In the book of Acts, we discover how the Holy Spirit worked and through whom He worked, as Jesus is building His Church. We find both the baptism *in* the Spirit for conversion taking place and the baptism *with* the Spirit for empowerment.

Let's examine a number of key Scriptures in Acts to help us understand more about Holy Spirit convergence.

■ **Acts 2:2-4**

"And suddenly there came from heaven a noise like a violent, rushing wind, and it filled the whole house where they were sitting. And there appeared to them tongues as of fire distributing themselves, and they rested on each one of them. And they were all <u>filled with the Holy Spirit</u> and began to <u>speak with other tongues</u>, as the Spirit was giving them utterance."

The Holy Spirit was sent by Jesus on the day of Pentecost or the day of first-fruits (Numbers 28:26) to continue the expansion of His Church. As previously mentioned, Jesus' Church began with the first believers after His resurrection and continued to grow during the forty days between His resurrection and ascension. Now, ten days after Jesus' ascension, the prophecy of Joel was fulfilled and there was a great harvest or ingathering of "first-fruits" from the Jews.

The believers, being obedient to Jesus' command to wait in Jerusalem, experienced this amazing convergence of the Holy Spirit on them beyond their conversion experience. This experience was accompanied by a loud sound that filled the place where they gathered, tongues or flames of fire upon them, and speaking in other tongues by the Holy Spirit.

This was a divine work exclusively! The NIV Study Bible points out that Acts 2:4 is, "A fulfillment of Acts 1:5,8; see also Jesus' promise in Luke 24:49. Their spirits were completely under the control of the Spirit; their words were his words." [6]

How did the speaking in other tongues as the Spirit gave them "utterance" or "enabled" (NIV) them, bring glory to God? Acts 2:11 reveals the answer – *"...we hear them in our own tongues speaking the mighty deeds of God."* Those Jews visiting Jerusalem from 15 different regions of the Roman Empire "heard" the Gospel in their language from Christ-followers who did not know all these languages! God's divine intervention is the only explanation.

We might ask, "Did the Holy Spirit enable the believers to each speak different foreign languages?" Think about it for a moment. If there were numerous believers speaking 15 different foreign languages all at the same time, they would have to yell above one another to be heard and it seems there would be mass confusion as a result.

But, if these believers spoke out a heavenly spiritual language as the Spirit enabled them and the Spirit intervened so that each of those foreigners "heard" the message in their own language, then this would be a God-glorifying work. Which it was!

Another reason I've come to the conclusion that the believers spoke in spiritual or heavenly tongues, not in foreign languages all at once, is that Scripture records -- *"But others were mocking and saying, 'They are full of sweet wine.' "* (Acts 2:13). Why would some accuse the believers of being drunk if they were speaking foreign languages that could be understood by those gathered there?

But, because they were speaking the language of the Spirit in "tongues", which may sound unintelligible, then it stands to reason that some would come to this conclusion that they were drunk.

Peter got up with the eleven other original Apostles and proclaimed – *"For these men are not drunk, as you suppose, for it is only the third hour of the day; but this is what was spoken of through the prophet Joel:"* (Acts 2:15-16). In other words, this was God's power, not man's foolishness. There was no confusion, just the Gospel revelation. As a result, people were *"...amazed and astonished, saying 'Why, are not all these who are speaking Galileans?"* (Acts 2:7).

Peter boldly revealed God's divine plan for all people. He was no longer the coward who had denied Jesus three times in the past, now he was transformed by the baptism *with* the Spirit. He spoke with courage and defended his faith.

The result was that those gathered to see what was happening asked, *"...Brethren, what shall we do?"* (Acts 2:37) These Jews who heard the truth of God came under the conviction of the Holy Spirit and *"were pierced to the heart"* (Acts 2:37), just as Jesus had explained earlier to His disciples prior to His death. Peter makes it clear that all are to *"...Repent and let each of you be baptized in the name of Jesus Christ for the forgiveness of your sins..."* (Acts 2:38). We would call this a "Come to Jesus time"! This was a time of baptism *in* the Spirit for conversion unto salvation.

Only by putting their faith in Jesus Christ for salvation would they then repent and be identified with Jesus through water baptism. That day about 3,000 people were saved and baptized. Again, an amazing convergence of the Spirit!

The main point is that the believers on Pentecost were filled and empowered by the Holy Spirit to do the work of

God. They saw evidence of God's supernatural intervention again into humanity. They served God's purpose to reach others with the message of Jesus. As Christ-followers, we are able to do the same.

■ **Acts 8:14-19**

"Now when the apostles in Jerusalem heard that Samaria had received the word of God, they sent them Peter and John, who came down and prayed for them, that they might receive the Holy Spirit. For He had not yet fallen upon any of them; they had simply been baptized in the name of the Lord Jesus. Then they began laying their hands on them, and they were receiving the Holy Spirit."

Through Philip the Evangelist, the Gospel of Jesus was brought to the Samarians. Many had come to faith in Jesus and were baptized in water. They were born-again by the Holy Spirit or baptized *in* the Holy Spirit.

When Peter and John came to inspect the evangelistic work taking place, they became aware that these new believers had not experienced the baptism *with* the Holy Spirit and that the Holy Spirit *"had not yet fallen upon any of them"* (v. 16). From their immediate observation of the situation, we can conclude that the Apostles recognized that this manifestation of the Holy Spirit after one's conversion to Jesus was a normal experience. Therefore, it was not just limited to the day of Pentecost, but was an on-going spiritual convergence experience.

I appreciate what the Spirit Filled Life Bible explains on this passage. The commentators state,

> "This passage has been subject to unnecessary debate. The sequence of events described in v. 12 leaves little doubt that the Samaritans had become Christians. They had already had a conversion experience with the Holy Spirit, evidenced by their water baptism (vv. 12, 16). Now, through the ministry of the apostles, they are being led into another significant experience with the Holy Spirit, which Luke describes both as 'receiving the Holy Spirit,' including their allowing Him to 'fall upon' them. This, therefore, may best be seen in the sense of their initial baptism with the Holy Spirit." [7]

This convergence work of the Spirit was not just for the Jews who were redeemed through Jesus, but now also the "half-Jews" or previously despised Samaritans. They were experiencing the grace and mercy of God unto salvation and Spirit-empowerment. Glory to God!

■ **Acts 9:4-6, 17-18**

"And he (Saul) fell to the ground and heard a voice saying to him, 'Saul, Saul, why are you

persecuting Me?' And he said, 'Who are You, Lord?' And He said, 'I am Jesus whom you are persecuting, but get up, and enter the city, and it will be told you what you must do…So Ananias departed and entered the house, and after laying his hands on him said, 'Brother Saul, the Lord Jesus, who appeared to you on the road by which you were coming, has sent me so that you may regain your sight, and be <u>filled with the Holy Spirit</u>. And immediately, there fell from his eyes something like scales and he regained his sight, and he got up and was baptized;"

Saul's conversion to Christ was dramatic! It is clear that he was converted during that moment he met Jesus on the road to Damascus. After being blind for three days, the Lord sent His servant, Ananias, to embrace Saul, lay hands on him and be an instrument in the impartation or filling *with* the Spirit. Notice that Ananias addresses Saul as **"Brother Saul",** a clear indication that Jesus revealed to him that Saul was now a believer and needed a further divine touch from God.

This can be seen as the Apostle Paul's commissioning into ministry, as well as his baptism *with* the Holy Spirit for empowerment in this ministry. We note that **"and immediately he began to proclaim Jesus in the synagogues, saying 'He is the Son of God'."** (Acts 9:20). The evidence of his heart-change, calling, and convergence experience through the Holy Spirit was evident in his boldness to declare Jesus openly and immediately.

■ **Acts 10:44-47**

"While Peter was still speaking these words, the Holy Spirit fell upon all those who were listening to the message. All the circumcised believers who came with Peter were amazed, because the <u>gift of the Holy Spirit</u> had been poured out upon the Gentiles also. For they were hearing them <u>speaking with tongues</u> and exalting God. Then Peter answered, 'Surely no one can refuse the water for these to be baptized who <u>have received the Holy Spirit just as we did</u>, can he?' "

It gets more and more exciting as the Holy Spirit continues working to the amazement of Peter and those Jews with him. First, the Holy Spirit comes upon Samaritan believers and now upon Gentile believers.

Peter had received a vision from the Lord and then was willing to accept the invitation to go to the home of Cornelius, the Roman centurion (see Acts 10:1). Cornelius was so excited at what God was doing that he invited his relatives and friends.

He was a person of influence and when Peter arrived he *"...found many people assembled."* (Acts 10:27). Then, as he declares the truth about Jesus to those gathered, a Holy Spirit convergence takes place!

The people gathered in Cornelius' home that day evidently had accepted Jesus by faith as they heard Peter speak of believing in Jesus to receive the forgiveness of sins. This was the first work of the Holy Spirit. Then, while Peter was still sharing, the second work of the Holy Spirit took place immediately following their believing.

We can't miss this – *"...the Holy Spirit fell upon all who were listening to the message."* (v. 44). There was clear evidence of this to Peter and the other Jews by the manifestation of *"speaking in tongues..."* (v. 46).

The Jewish believers who had also come *"were amazed, because the gift of the Holy Spirit had been poured out on the Gentiles also."* (v. 45). This was a divine work of God happening in their midst, and it involved non-Jews. It included the additional empowerment and impartation of the Spirit through a visible manifestation – speaking in tongues.

As Peter will later testify – *"The Lord is not slow about His promise, as some count slowness, but is patient toward you, not wishing for any to perish but for all to come to repentance."* (II Peter 3:9). Jesus was doing a work in Peter, as a Jew, as well as in Cornelius, a Roman Gentile. The kingdom of God is expanding through the work of the Holy Spirit and His empowerment.

We should never underestimate who the Holy Spirit may move upon or how He may choose to do it. When you are sharing Jesus with others, expect Him to be touching their heart.

■ **Acts 11:15-17**

*"And as I began to speak, <u>the Holy Spirit fell</u>
<u>upon them</u> just as He did upon us at the
beginning. And I remembered the word of the
Lord, how He used to say, 'John baptized with
water, but you shall be <u>baptized with the Holy</u>
<u>Spirit.</u>' Therefore if God gave to them <u>the same</u>
<u>gift</u> as He gave us also after believing in the Lord
Jesus Christ, who was I that I could stand in
God's way?"*

Peter explains to those back in Jerusalem what took
place among the Gentiles. He confirms this work of the
Holy Spirit by referring to the words Jesus had spoken to
him and the other disciples earlier. This convergence of the
Spirit was again proof that Jesus is the Baptizer *with* the
Holy Spirit after conversion.

Peter points out that the same manifestation of the
Spirit that took place on them at Pentecost, with the
speaking in tongues, also occurred with these Gentile
believers. Peter had all the proof needed and he didn't
want to be a hindrance to the work of God or oppose God.
It was a wonderful work of the Holy Spirit and who would
want to stand in God's way?

■ **Acts 19:1-7**

"It happened that while Apollos was at Corinth, Paul passed through the upper country and came to Ephesus, and found some disciples. He said to them, 'Did you receive the Holy Spirit when you believed?' And they said to him, 'No, we have not even heard whether there is a Holy Spirit.' And he said, 'Into what then where you baptized?' And they said, 'Into John's baptism'. Paul said, 'John baptized with the baptism of repentance, telling the people to believe in Him who was coming after him, that is, in Jesus.' When they heard this, they were baptized into the name of the Lord Jesus. And when Paul had laid his hands upon them, <u>the Holy Spirit came on them</u>, and they began <u>speaking with tongues and prophesying</u>." There were in all about twelve men."

The Lord loves to put people on the right track – the truth track! Often, we operate on limited knowledge or information and God wants to do more. Such was the case when Paul encountered these twelve disciples, who did not have the full revelation of God's work.

<u>The NIV Study Bible</u> commentary points out regarding *"some disciples"* that -- "These 12 (v. 7) seem to have been followers of Jesus, but indirectly through John the Baptist or some of his followers. Or perhaps they had received

their teaching from Apollos himself in his earlier state of partial understanding (see 18:26). Like Apollos, they had a limited understanding of the gospel." [8]

Therefore, they were ignorant of the full will and work of God. Paul informs them correctly and administers believer's water baptism in the name of the Lord Jesus. It can be assumed from the text that after they were immersed, Paul then placed his hands on them and prayed for the baptism *with* the Holy Spirit to be imparted. There was a clear manifestation that resulted.

This is revealed clearly to us by the fact that those whom Paul laid hands on, *"the Holy Spirit came on them"* (v. 6). The promise of the Father was imparted by Jesus through the Holy Spirit and there was the manifestation of speaking in tongues and prophesying.

No one could deny what had happened in this convergence experience. It was the same experience as on the Day of Pentecost with the 120 believers, among the Samaritan believers, and then the Gentile believers.

The acts of the Holy Spirit are evident among those being reached with the Gospel of Jesus Christ in the first century Church. Every century since has seen the continued work of the Holy Spirit to build Jesus' Church. He is doing the will of the Father and Jesus, to our benefit and to bring in God's harvest.

It is important not to confuse the baptism *with* the Spirit and other references regarding His work in the body Christ. One such reference is found in Ephesians 4:3-6:

"being diligent to preserve the unity of the Spirit in the bond of peace. There is one body and one Spirit, just as also you were called in one hope of your calling; one Lord, one faith, one baptism, one God and Father of all who is over all and through all and in all."

The NIV Study Bible notes with regard to the phrase *"one baptism"* (v. 5) – "Probably not the baptism of the Spirit (see I Co 12:13), which was inward and therefore invisible, but water baptism. Since Paul apparently has in mind that which identifies all believers as belonging together, he would naturally refer to that church ordinance in which every new convert participated publicly." [9]

In I Corinthians 12:12-13, the apostle Paul points out that:

"For even as the body is one and yet has many members, and all the members of the body, though they are many, are one body, so also is Christ. For <u>by</u> the one Spirit we were all baptized into one body, whether Jews or Greeks, whether slaves or free, and we were all made to drink of the one Spirit."

The text reveals for us that this specific baptism *"by"* the Holy Spirit is dealing with being born-again or conversion to Christ. This is the only way a person becomes part of the body of Christ.

The NIV Study Bible explains regarding the phrase – *"all baptized by one Spirit into one body"* that this denotes, "Spiritually baptized, regenerated by the Holy Spirit (Jn.3:3,5) and united with Christ as part of his body." [10]

The phrase, *"all given the one Spirit to drink"* refers to "God has given all his people the Holy Spirit to indwell them (6:19) so that their lives may overflow with the fruit of the Spirit (Gal. 5:22-23; cf Jn.7:37-39)." [11]

Here we discover the Apostle Paul revealing that those baptized by the one Spirit into one body, is about being immersed into Christ and His Church as true believers through the internal work of the Spirit. This is the first convergence of the Spirit with our eternal spirit. This is where our relationship with Jesus begins. As mentioned before, we must differentiate between the baptism *of* the Spirit and the baptism *with* the Spirit. The baptism *of* the Spirit must come first and involves our salvation, which is eternal. The baptism *with* the Spirit is for temporal empowerment.

For clarification, we must remember what the Apostle Paul tells us in I Corinthians 13:8-10:

"Love never fails; but if there are gifts of prophecy, they will be done away with; if there are tongues, they will cease; and if there is knowledge, it will be done away. For we know in part and we prophesy in part; but when the perfect comes, the partial will be done away."

When Christ returns in glory, *"the perfect"* or perfection will also come! This is what we look forward to, but until that great and glorious Day, we must allow the Holy Spirit to work His work in and through us. We should not grieve or resist the Spirit, but allow Him to keep filling us. We should allow Him to enable us with speaking in tongues, either devotionally, in intercession, or publicly for the edification of the church.

We should be open to the Spirit bringing prophecy through us to build up and encourage others. These are valid today, just as *"knowledge"* (v. 8) of God is valid today. The return of Christ will bring completion and full revelation of the secret things of God.

Before concluding this chapter, I feel it is helpful for our understanding to let Scripture confirm Scripture, which is what I have sought to do. There is one more foundational passage that is very insightful for us on this subject of the baptism *with* the Spirit. This Scripture is Hebrews 6:1-2 (NIV), which states:

> *"Therefore let us leave the elementary teachings about Christ and go on to maturity, not laying again the foundation of repentance from acts that lead to death, and of faith in God, instructions about <u>baptisms</u>, the laying on of hands, the resurrection of the dead, and eternal judgment."*

Here the writer of Hebrews informs us of the *"principles of the doctrine of Christ"* (KJV); *"elementary principles of Christ"* (NKJV); or *"elementary teachings about Christ"* (NIV/NASB). These teachings or doctrines are what the early church proclaimed and lived under as the truth of God.

We note that one of these teachings is regarding *"baptisms"* – more than one type of baptism. The believers in Christ after His resurrection were familiar with two specific baptisms. The first being the command of Jesus in Matthew 28:19, which is believer's water baptism. The second is what Jesus informed His followers of in Acts 1:5 – baptism *with* the Holy Spirit.

The first is for identification *with* Christ and the second is for empowerment *from* Christ.

These were both experienced at the beginning of the Church, as well as afterward through the growth of the Church.

The *"laying on of hands"* is also mentioned in Hebrews 6 as a foundational teaching. One purpose was for an impartation of the filling of the Spirit, as noted previously in the book of Acts.

II Timothy 1:6 shows us that the laying on of hands was also for an impartation of ministry gifting or calling. The NIV Study Bible notes – "Paul was God's instrument, through whom the gift came from the Holy Spirit to Timothy." [12]

Until Jesus returns, we should embrace, teach, and practice all six of these essential doctrines of Christ. I believe this is clearly His will for His Church of all ages.

Chapter 11 – Fulfilling the Great Assignment

Congratulations! You've made it through a lot of Scripture references revealing the convergence of the Holy Spirit in the lives of many different people over the span of thousands of years.

His work continues today in a dynamic manner and is connected to what I call "The Great Assignment" that Jesus gave His followers in Matthew 28:18-20:

> *"And Jesus came up and spoke to them, saying, 'All authority has been given to Me in heaven and on earth. Go therefore and make disciples of all the nations, baptizing them in the name of the Father and the Son and the Holy Spirit, teaching them to observe all that I have commanded you; and lo, I am with you always, even to the end of the age.' "*

There are various ways the Holy Spirit worked in the lives of the early believers to fulfill this assignment of Jesus during their lifetime. Let's examine some of these to encourage us in our personal life, ministry, or mission outreach.

The Dynamic Leading of the Spirit

In Acts 8 we find one of the unique ways in which the Holy Spirit works in and through Christ-followers. There are four matters to examine here taken from the experience of Philip.

The Samaritan Revival (Acts 8:1-8)

Philip had been chosen to be a servant-leader or deacon in the Jerusalem church to assist with the basic needs among the believers (see Acts 6:3-5). He was a servant at heart and willing to care for people in need. God loves to use people who have the humble, obedient spirit of servant-hood.

When the early believers faced persecution, there were many who left Jerusalem and were led to other parts of the region. Scripture tells us that they *"went about preaching the word"* (Acts 8:4). Philip was among those who were called out. His ministry was enlarged from being a deacon to serving in the ministry gift of evangelist. The Holy Spirit called him from serving physical food to proclaiming Christ as the "Bread of Life".

He was led to Samaria and the people there received the truth he spoke about Jesus. In fact, a revival broke out in one of the cities, most likely the capital city.

We see the dynamic work of the Holy Spirit taking place, which included miraculous signs, people being delivered of evil spirits, as well as, many paralytics and cripples being healed. God was at work as Christ was proclaimed through this servant, Philip.

The Holy Spirit may be leading you to a particular city or region to share Jesus. Maybe the circumstances are not what you expected. Can the Holy Spirit still use you? If you have a servant's heart and a desire to declare the love of Christ, you can expect Him to open a door of opportunity. Keep in mind that His ways are above our ways. We see that with Philip.

The Confusing Call (Acts 8:26)

After a period of time, something unusual occurs. We are told, *"But an angel of the Lord spoke to Philip saying, 'Get up and go south to the road that descends from Jerusalem to Gaza.' (This is a desert road.)"* (Acts 8:26).

Doesn't it seem odd that God would move Philip from a great revival in Samaria with many people being impacted, to go into the desert where few are found?

We would say, "There's something wrong with this picture." Doesn't God want as many to be saved and enter His kingdom as possible? If so, the evangelist should stay in the city and keep the crusade going! This just doesn't seem logical or reasonable from our perspective. But, the Lord is the One who sees the big picture...the whole picture of reaching a lost world.

Philip was faced with the challenge of trusting the Lord in this, even though it didn't seem like the right time to make a move, especially out to the desert.

We too, are often challenged with hearing and trusting the Lord to make certain moves. We may feel very comfortable in a situation and it may appear like we are having an impact on people, when the Lord calls us to follow Him in a different manner, to a different place or type of ministry. It may be out of our "comfort zone", but completely within God's kingdom plan for our lives. Will we trust Him and His leading by the Holy Spirit?

Francis Chan points out the following:

"There is a real difference between adding the Holy Spirit to your life and actually following Him minute by minute. If you add the Spirit to your life, you're not open to change; you just want to enhance what you're already doing. This is not what the Spirit came to do. On the other hand, if you begin following the Spirit's leading in your life, you will find yourself changing. The Spirit may prompt you to let go of things that were once important to you. He may even call you to give up some things in your life, at least for a time, in order to accomplish His purposes in and through you." [1]

The Divine Appointment (Acts 8:27-35)

Look what Philip did – *"So he got up and went..."* (Acts 8:27). Isn't it always the first step of obedience that is the hardest step? It is for me. Philip knew the Lord and trusted the Lord to do His work, His way. We need the help of the Helper, the Holy Spirit, to do the same in our daily life and ministry. We need to get up and go also.

Interestingly, Philip just "happened" to meet someone out in the desert as he was walking by faith in obedience. He met an Ethiopian official, in charge of the treasury of Candace, queen of the Ethiopians. This man had been in Jerusalem and was on his way back to Ethiopia. There must have been quite a caravan accompanying him, for he was an important official.

Was this just by chance? No way! The Lord re-positioned Philip for a purpose – to meet this official while he was traveling, before he left the country. It was a divine appointment and convergence connection.

Now we discover what's really going on – *"Then the Spirit said to Philip, 'Go up and join this chariot' "* (Acts 8: 29). The Holy Spirit had been working through Philip in the past and now gave him a direct command – *"Go..."*!

It's the same as when Jesus told His followers just prior to His ascension – *"Go..."* (Matthew 28:19). I believe that the two letters – "GO" represent two words – "Get Out". The Lord wants us to get out and declare Him to others. Later, I'll share some specific ways the Spirit called me to "get out" in ministry in order to fulfill His assignments.

When Philip *"ran up"* (Acts 8:30) to the chariot, he heard what the man was reading. It was from the book of Isaiah, the prophet. What perfect timing!

Philip could have reasoned that since the man was reading the Scriptures, the Holy Spirit would reveal to him the truth and everything would be fine. But, this man was confused, like so many we encounter in our world. Instead, Philip took the opportunity to get personally involved with the man. Philip asked one very simple question – *"Do you understand what you are reading?"* (Acts 8:30). Philip was building a bridge relationally by asking this question with the intent of speaking truth into the man's life.

When Philip was invited to *"come up and sit with him"* (Acts 8:31), he realized just what the Holy Spirit had been doing. The man was reading Isaiah 53:7-8, which is a prophetic revelation about the Messiah. The Ethiopian man was sincere in wanting to know the truth being revealed by the prophet Isaiah and who better to tell him than Philip?

The story unfolds – *"Then Philip opened his mouth, and beginning from this Scripture he preached Jesus to him."* (Acts 8:35). The Holy Spirit had prepared this man's heart and also led Philip to an opportunity to share Jesus from his own experience. How awesome is that?

Philip most likely shared "Who" Jesus is, "why" He came, and "what" He did. It was plain and simple! That's why it is so important that we know Jesus personally, walk with Him each day, and then seek for how the Holy Spirit would have us share Him.

Looking back on the CDTS experience again, brings to mind the mission of YWAM – "To know Him and make Him known". This is what Christ-followers are to be about, whether at home, in school, at work, in the community or on the mission field.

The Expansion of the Gospel (Acts 8:36-40)

The Ethiopian man opened his heart to Jesus by the power of the Holy Spirit and was born-again by faith. This is evident from his confession, *"I believe that Jesus Christ is the Son of God"* (Acts 8:37) and his request to be baptized. Philip certainly wouldn't have followed through if he questioned the man's salvation experience. It was a his initial Holy Spirit convergence experience. We read next, *"and they both went down into the water, Philip as well as the eunuch, and he baptized him."* (Acts 8:38).

This was a glorious day! The mission was accomplished concerning God's plan for Philip being in the desert. Then we read – *"the Spirit of the Lord snatched Philip away; and the eunuch no longer saw him..."* (Acts 8:39).

The Holy Spirit can and does act in mysterious ways. This is one of them. He moved Philip on to the next kingdom assignment. The important thing here is that the Ethiopian official *"...went on his way rejoicing."* (Acts 8:39). Salvation in Jesus causes people to rejoice, along with the angels in Heaven.

Now, do you think that this high official kept all this to himself? I don't believe so. When a person has the joy of the Lord, it is hard to contain it. I believe it was in God's plan for this man to tell his family, the queen of Ethiopia, her court and others in his sphere of influence.

Philip may have thought he was going to stay in Samaria to transform a city, but Jesus wanted him to be part of transforming a nation!

For each one of us, it doesn't matter how old we are or how much training we've had, Jesus wants to know if we are available to *"Go..."*.

Philip, the deacon, was available to serve where and when he was needed. The Spirit led him to where Jesus wanted him to go later when his Jerusalem assignment was done. Are you willing to do the same? It may be to impact a neighborhood, a school, a city, a state, or a nation. God knows and that should be enough.

While in the Philippines on Outreach with YWAM, our team was introduced to a book by an American missionary serving in Manila. The book is, I Want to Bear Fruit, by Chuck Quinley, with the sub-title: "YOU CAN LEARN TO BEAR FRUIT FOR GOD WITHOUT PRESSURING OTHERS OR EMBARRASSING YOURSELF".

Chuck takes to heart what Jesus said in John 15:16 (NIV):

"Jesus said, 'You did not choose me, but I chose you and appointed you to go and bear

fruit – fruit that will last. Then my Father will give you whatever you ask in my name.' "

He encourages believers to take four simple steps each day to bear fruit in the kingdom of God. He challenges people to covenant with God to do the following:

1. **Pray every morning**:   "Lord, today, send me someone who needs your help."

2. **Tune into others**: ask follow-up questions, listen carefully. Someone will tell you about a personal problem. That's your green light.

3. **Brag on Jesus**: tell them what he has done for you and for others. Tell them that he loves them and has a plan for their life and wants to reveal himself to them to prove he's real.

4. **Offer to pray for them on the spot**: this fixes it in their mind as an unusual God-event, and provides a chance for God's power to flow into them. [2]

I believe that Philip was asking the Spirit to send people to him to pray for and share Jesus with. That's why the Lord took him to the desert for this very important convergence encounter.

When the opportunity came, there was no pressure applied, Philip simply obeyed the Spirit and asked the official a simple question – *"Do you understand what you are reading?"* or "How can I help you?" Most people are open to help when they are confused or in crisis.

Are we willing to also be servants of Jesus and make ourselves available to people in need spiritually, emotionally, or physically? I've discovered in my years of ministry that people are often willing to change when going through a crisis in their life. We need to meet them where they are at and offer hope.

The Holy Spirit will set up the divine appointments if we are willing. Spiritual fruit will come because He is at work. And always remember, He does the saving. He chooses to work through us because Jesus has *"appointed"* us to *"go and bear fruit"* for Him. His heart is to have *"fruit that will last"*, the eternal fruit of redeemed lives.

This was also the heart and motivation of the Apostle Paul. He states in I Corinthians 9:22-23:

"To the weak I became weak, that I might win the weak; I have become all things to all men, so that I may by all means save some. I do all things for the sake of the gospel, so that I may become a fellow partaker of it."

What a joy to be a *"fellow partaker"* of the gospel of Jesus, the risen and living One. We too, should seek through the Holy Spirit, to reach people where they are at.

When I first moved to Seattle to serve as NW Area Director of CBN Ministries, I encountered a group of pastors who wanted to bear fruit for Jesus outside their regular sphere of influence.

One Christmas, as a ministry leader in the city, I was offered cases of beautiful Christmas booklets from Campus Crusade for Christ. They were very well done and the last pages presented the gospel very clearly. I asked the Holy Spirit how these could be sown into the city in a way that people would accept them.

He showed me a unique, non-threatening way to do it. I was to ask several other pastors to dress up with me as the Dicken's Carolers and go to Pike St. Market in downtown Seattle. There we would sing Christmas carols on the sidewalk. As we attracted a crowd of people with our costumes and singing, we were to simply offer those who gathered around us one of the Christmas booklets.

I knew of a local church had these costumes – black top hats, black capes, and colorful scarves. We dressed the part, joined in prayer, took our Christmas song books, and headed for the most popular corner of the city by the market. As we began singing, people began gathering and I began handing out the booklets. People were elated to get one of these special gifts. I observed people crossing the street just to come over and get their own Christmas booklet.

The cases of Christmas booklets were "Gospel seeds" sown into the lives of many people and homes that day. It was creative, simple, and exciting. I keep a picture of the four Dicken's Carolers at Pike St. Market in my office as a reminder that the Spirit loves to use special means to reach a lost world for Jesus.

The next Christmas, a fellow pastor asked me to share this with his church evangelism team and take people from his church to the streets. There were about twenty-five in this "caroling choir" from that church who came. This time we went to the shopping area in the heart of Seattle. It was crowded with many shoppers and very festive. The same thing happened – as we sang the Christmas carols people gathered around and listened.

We had several who walked through the crowd and gave away the booklets as gifts to hundreds of people. It was a great way to get God's people out on the streets and the Gospel out to people drawn in by a special occasion. This is what it means to *"Go..."* – get out and reach out!

Francis Chan states: "Without the supernatural power of God in our lives, we remain incredibly ordinary. Our churches remain ordinary." [3]

Ask the Spirit how He desires to use you and your church to share Jesus with the world.

Impacting Empowerment

We can each learn something valuable from how others faced great challenges in following Jesus faithfully. I have been greatly strengthened by what took place among the first believers not too long after Pentecost. There was a crisis in the Jerusalem church. This crisis was huge and very threatening to everyone.

Acts 4 reveals that Peter and John were arrested upon the order of the Jewish religious leaders because the apostles *"...were teaching the people and proclaiming in Jesus the resurrection of the dead."* (Acts 4:2). When they were called before the Sanhedrin to be judged and punished we read, *"Then Peter, filled with the Holy Spirit, said to them..."* (Acts 4:8). Peter was not the same person who had denied Jesus three times at His trial. Peter had changed! He no longer had fear of the Jewish leaders, but was empowered through faith in Jesus and the anointing power of the Holy Spirit.

Peter boldly declared to these religious leaders that, *"...there is salvation in no one else; for there is no other name under heaven that has been given among men, by which we must be saved."* (Acts 4:12). These leaders saw the courage of these two disciples and *"...began to recognize them as having been with Jesus."* (Acts 4:13). Isn't it amazing how the influence of Jesus brought about a whole different priority in these disciples lives? They were ready and willing to be martyrs for Jesus and the Gospel.

This was apparent when they were *"commanded"* (Acts 4:18) not to declare Jesus or teach about Him any-more. Their response was the same as ours should be:

"...Whether it is right in the sight of God to give heed to you rather than God, you be the judge; for we cannot stop speaking about what we have seen and heard." (vv. 19-20)

Do you see the effect the filling of the Spirit has? It replaces fear with faith. We are willing to surrender all to Jesus to declare His name. We are willing to testify to what we know to be true, whether anyone else agrees or not.

I personally wonder if Peter and John shared with each other, before coming to trial, the words they knew to be true from Zechariah 4:6:

> **"...Not by might, nor by power, but by My Spirit, says the LORD of hosts.' "**.

They knew the Old Testament Scriptures well and the Holy Spirit may have brought it to their remembrance at this challenging time. Remember, the Apostles faced the same Jewish council that condemned Jesus and had Him crucified. They faced the same possibility.

A verse like this may be used by the Lord to hold us up and move us forward when we are threatened or overwhelmed in ministry. The Lord is Sovereign and His might and power will prevail through the Holy Spirit.

When Peter and John were released, they returned to the believers and gave a report of all that happened, including the command not to declare Jesus. Knowing the severity of the situation at hand, the Apostles called for specific prayer that would first, turn their trust toward God and second, release their faith so as to increase their scope of witness.

As they *"...lifted their voices to God with one accord..."* (Acts 4:24), we find an important revelation in how they addressed God. The believers acknowledge the power and might of God by beginning with – *"Sovereign Lord..."* (Acts 4:24 NIV). When we face a crisis, we too should acknowledge Who God is and the power He has.

When we take our eyes off ourselves and our situation and surrender to the Sovereign One, we will recognize that He is also the All-Sufficient One!

In their prayer, the believers also made reference to the work of the Holy Spirit in King David and what he prophesied many years prior (Acts 4:25-26).

Note further what these faithful believers asked for in their prayer:

"And now, Lord, take note of their threats and grant that Your bond-servants may speak Your word with confidence, while You extend Your hand to heal, and signs and wonders take place through the name of Your holy servant Jesus." (Acts 4:29-30)

They didn't ask to be spared persecution and suffering, but instead to be empowered or enabled to carry on as Jesus had commanded in the great assignment (Matthew 28:18-20).

Before His ascension, Jesus delegated His authority to His followers and commissioned them to go and declare Him to all the world, regardless of the threats that would come against them. He even told them that He was sending them out as sheep among wolves, meaning that there would be hardships ahead.

These believers wanted more! They sought more of the Spirit's power and might to speak boldly and with confidence. They wanted God to do more. More healings, miracles, and signs and wonders, to be evidence to their family, friends, neighbors, and anyone else of Who Jesus is. They wanted more of Jesus to be exalted and lifted up to the world, including the religious leaders who were threatening them. In essence, their prayer request was simply – "More Lord!" That's a good one for us to pray in challenging situations – "More of You, Lord. More of Your awesome power at work in me for Your glory."

There is more that transpires when these believers exercised their faith in God through heart-felt prayer. There are numerous supernatural aspects that occurred through the work of the Holy Spirit. Let's take special note of these. They are as follows:

■ A Supernatural Encounter (Acts 4:31)

"And when they had prayed, the place where they had gathered was shaken…"

God shook the house! This was not a natural happening like an earthquake, this was a "Spirit-quake". This was a physical manifestation of God's Presence. The Lord was answering their prayer and showed up to intervene in their lives.

We must always remember that God is aware of every situation in our lives; nothing takes Him by surprise. He desires to intervene when we call upon Him.

■ A Supernatural Fullness (Acts 4:31)

"...and they were all filled with the Holy Spirit..."

Everyone present experienced a filling *"with the Holy Spirit"*.

These were all believers in Jesus, saved people, who were seeking more of God. This outpouring or manifestation of the Spirit was to enable them to do what they had been requesting. This is God's work to keep His people moving forward. He calls us to "advance" by the power of the Spirit.

■ A Supernatural Boldness (Acts 4:31)

"...and began to speak the word of God with boldness."

Their prayer of faith led to a divine filling that resulted in a fearlessness to proclaim the revelation of God. They spoke or declared the truth of God and were determined to be obedient, even unto death.

In Acts 1:8, Jesus tells His followers that they will receive power through the Holy Spirit, and He informs them *"...and you shall be My witnesses...to the remotest part of the earth."* The Greek word for "witnesses" comes from the root word for "martyr". They are directly connected. Jesus was telling those who wanted to be His disciples to prepare to give their life, not just spiritually, but also physically. We must lay down our life completely to be a faithful follower.

This action of declaring the Word of God boldly was in direct violation of what the Jewish leaders had ordered. It is obvious that the believers had the conviction of obeying God rather than man. Revelation 12:11 tells us, *"...and they did not love their life even when faced with death."*

This is the supreme test of a Christ-follower. The test becomes a testimony to others when there is obedience, especially to those of the generations to come. Fox's Book of Martyrs attests to this fact. It reveals many who followed Jesus into martyrdom. It is a true inspiration to us today.

Francis Chan notes – "It is impossible to encounter the Holy Spirit of God and not be changed." [4]

■ A Supernatural Unity (Acts 4:32)

"And the congregation of those who believed were of one heart and soul..."

The Lord desires for there to be unity in His Body. Among these early believers, we discover that with the filling of the Holy Spirit, the fellowship was unified.

What a blessing when a team or church are of one heart and soul!

When we seek God and pray together for His will to be done, there should be a divine unity that takes place. Sad to say, this is often rare because of certain personalities, personal agendas, or spiritual immaturity that interferes.

The outcome of genuine unity among God's people is reveled in Psalm 133, *"...For there the LORD command-ed the blessing – life forever."* (Psalm 133:3). This unity is what Jesus prayed for in the Garden of Gethsemane, recorded in John 17:23 (NIV) – *"May they be brought to complete unity to let the world know that you sent me...".*

This unity is what the Apostle Paul expresses in Philippians 2:2-3:

"...make my joy complete by being of the same mind, maintaining the same love, united in spirit, intent on one purpose. Do nothing from selfishness or empty conceit, but with humility of mind regard one another as more important than yourselves;"

This is a high calling – unity – one that was evident in the early church through the Holy Spirit. He wants you to play your part in unifying others. This takes continual effort and the help of the Spirit.

■ A Supernatural Submission (Acts 4:32)

"...and not one of them claimed that anything belonging to him was his own, but all things were common property to them."

It is obvious here that they were submitted to God, to the Apostles as leaders, and to each other. This generous sharing is a testimony of that. They were yielded to the Spirit and allowed the Him to guide them and provide for them in their particular circumstances at that time.

I feel that when we are fully submitted to the Lord and those in spiritual leadership who are led by the Word and Spirit of God, there will be blessings that follow.

■ A Supernatural Testimony (Acts 4:33)

"And with great power the apostles were giving testimony to the resurrection of the Lord Jesus..."

The truth about Jesus' resurrection was ramped up!
More than before did the Apostles take opportunity to testify to the truth of Jesus. It was given with ***"great power"*** as a witness that it was undeniable.

We have that same testimony. As believers we know the eternal difference that the resurrection of our Lord Jesus has made in us. Let's be bold in sharing it with those who still need to know.

■ A Supernatural Grace (Acts 4:33)

"...and abundant grace was upon them all."

With a renewed empowerment there was a new zeal to reach people for Christ and fulfill the great assignment. Jesus had a plan and it was being implemented through these early believers. Not only was the power of God manifest through the leaders, but we are told – ***"abundant grace was upon them all"***.

Don't you love hearing this? When the Holy Spirit is allowed to work in a fellowship, there will be ***"abundant grace"*** among those who are a part of it. When there is little or no grace for each other, it's a pretty good indication that the "traditions of men" have become a stronghold or that a self-righteous, legalistic, or controlling attitude is surfacing.

We are well aware that Jesus was ***"...full of grace and truth"*** (John 1:14) and ***"...of His fullness we have all received grace upon grace."*** (John 1:16). Are we reflecting Him in our relationships?

We will see fruitfulness when we operate in the same manner that He did through the Spirit. Is God's grace flowing through you into the lives of others? If so, how is this evident? Do you have grace for some, but not for others in the fellowship of believers? How can the Holy Spirit help you be more like Jesus in this area? It will affect our testimony one way or the other.

■ A Supernatural Generosity (Acts 4:34-35)

"For there was not a needy person among them,
for all who were owners of land or houses would
sell them and bring the proceeds of the sales,
and lay them at the apostle's feet; and they would be
distributed to each, as any had need."

This extreme generosity is evident by the fact that, *"there was not a needy person among them."* It is apparent that faith had increased and love was abounding among these believers. A spirit of sacrifice and generosity was evident in their midst through the work of the Holy Spirit. When the Spirit calls you by faith to sow into the lives of others, trust Him.

We must always remember that when we give out of a spirit of generosity, it's not the amount but the motive that matters. The joy of the Lord must be evident in our generous giving. Do we truly believe that everything we have belongs to the Lord? Then, we will yield to His leading.

Generosity comes from a heart that trusts God and seeks to bless others in His name. This is a spiritual investment that makes a difference, bringing God glory. The witness of these faith-filled and obedient people still speaks to us today.

Radical Servants

Jesus set the example for the original disciples when He washed their dirty feet while in the upper room where they ate the Passover meal prior to His arrest. It was a "teaching moment" that would remain in their minds as they continued Jesus' ministry after His ascension.

With the expansion of the church in Jerusalem after Pentecost, there were some challenges that needed to be dealt with, mainly the *"daily serving of food"* (Acts 6:1) to those in need. The Apostles realized it was time to delegate ministry to others to meet the need that they were not capable of handling. The apparent need was for people to *"serve tables"* (Acts 6:2). It involved serving individuals with care and compassion.

Who did they need to put in charge of the church "serving ministry"? Those who were *"of good reputation, full of the Spirit and of wisdom"* (Acts 6:3). There were certain distinct qualifications to being commissioned to serve others.

In his book, "Spirit Rising – Tapping into the Power of the Holy Spirit", Jim Cymbala notes the following on this matter of being qualified to serve,

> "Handing out food was a straightforward menial task, yet the apostles felt that being full of or controlled by the Spirit was a necessary qualification to wisely handle that simple job. Compare that with some of our contemporary

church hiring practices. When selecting people for professional ministry positions, we usually look first for educational qualifications. Folks who have earned a seminary degree become prime candidates to lead Christ's people without anyone having first discerned whether these potential leaders show evidence of being controlled by the Spirit…but in the New Testament church, even the job of distributing food to widows required leaders who were Spirit-controlled and full of wisdom." [5]

Cymbala further comments on this saying,

"If all believers were full of the Holy Spirit, if everyone in the community were Spirit-controlled, the apostles wouldn't have laid down such a qualification. In fact, it would be downright silly…Being a Christian does not necessarily guarantee that a person lives a life controlled by the Spirit." [6]

We can conclude that radical serving by radical servants was God's will at the beginning of the Church and it still is today.

I want to again reference and bring to your attention what the Apostle Paul makes this clear in Ephesians 5:15-18:

"Therefore be very careful how you walk, not as unwise men but as wise, making the most of your time, because the days are evil. So then do not be

foolish, but understand what the will of the Lord is. And do not get drunk with wine, for that is dissipation, but <u>be filled with the Spirit.</u>"

How do we make the most of our time or *"every opportunity"* (Ephesians 5:16 NIV) to be radical servants of Jesus? By being *"filled with the Spirit"*! Paul is pointing out that if we are not under the influence of the Spirit, we will function in the flesh and miss the will of God.

The wise Christ-follower, turns away from the foolishness of the world. If we truly understand *"what the will of the Lord is"*, we will desire to be controlled or influenced by the Holy Spirit in every matter, especially serving others in Jesus' name.

Cymbala notes the following on this matter of Paul calling believers to *"be filled with the Spirit"*:

> "If all Christians were already filled with the Spirit at all times, why would there be this strong command from Paul...It seems that Paul was saying we need to keep on being controlled by the Spirit if we want to live wisely, to understand the Lord's will for our lives, and to make the most of every opportunity. If we're not Spirit-controlled, we will miss out on being what God wants us to be." [7]

So what would keep us from being Spirit-controlled? For some, it may be the fear of losing control. They still want life to go their way. There is a fear of where the Holy

Spirit may lead them or what He may do with them.

For others, it may be pride. They have achieved a level of status and being under the control of the Spirit may mean doing some "menial" job – like serving food and cleaning up after others.

Then, for others it may be that they are ignorant. Ignorant of what it truly means when Jesus states, *"If anyone wishes to come after Me, he must deny himself, and take up his cross and follow Me."* (Matthew 16:24). It may be that the church they grew up in didn't teach on true discipleship or the work of the Holy Spirit. As a result, they have a limited view or understanding of God's will to live sacrificially as a disciple of Christ.

Being a radical servant is important to Jesus. It involves full surrender, something many Christians resist today. I am so thankful that when Vivian and I attended the CDTS, we were each given specific areas to serve in during the week.

I recall that some in our class were "challenged" when they got their work assignment for the first part of the school. For them it meant getting up early to prepare breakfast for the mission base and they were not "morning people".

Others had work in the grounds-keeping area and were not used to a lot of manual labor. Others had dish washing duties after dinner. I and a classmate shared the respon-sibility of cleaning out and washing the two vans every day, as well as, transporting students to area stores on a regular schedule. This was all about being a servant and submitting to our leaders to meet the on-going needs of the ministry.

This was servant-hood "test" time. I had a Master's degree at the time, had served as pastor in three churches, had been the NW Director of a major national ministry with multiple staff, both paid and volunteer. And now, I had the privilege of vacuuming sand out of the carpet of dirty vans that had been on various outreaches, washing mud off the wheels and transporting fellow-students to where they wanted to go in the evening.

The joy in the serving comes when the Spirit is allowed to control, even in the menial tasks of ministry. When we stop allowing Him to use us as servants in every situation, we start resisting His influence and work. We should NEVER get to a place where we won't serve if we are able. It really is a heart matter. We will be "tested" on this all life-long. We need to be wise and follow our Master's example.

I appreciate so much the insight of Francis Chan when he shares:

"The Spirit wants to do more than just help us out a bit. He wants to transform us, patiently and steadily, into people who transform our corners of the world. We sometimes get so caught up in everything God wants us to do that we lose sight of who God wants us to be. The difference is significant. God wants us to be the type of people who love Him wholeheartedly, who depend on the Holy Spirit, who by faith reach out to the people around us. As we spend time pursuing God and enjoying the fellowship of the Spirit, we will begin to see our lives changing from the inside out." [8]

Read that insight over again. When we are truly the type of people God wants us to be, we will whole-heartedly do what God wants us to do. Don't you agree?

Great Assignment Ministry

The Holy Spirit is continually prompting and leading Christ-followers in new ways to fulfill The Great Assignment (or Great Commission) given to us. In each unique situation, He desires to work His work.

I am inspired by the words of Isaiah 42:9 –

> *"Behold, the former things have come to pass,*
> *Now I declare new things,*
> *Before they spring forth I proclaim them to you."*

I'd like to encourage you with some ways the Holy Spirit has led me and others to participate in bringing in Jesus' harvest.

THE BIBLE GIVE-AWAY

In several churches that I have served, we have given away many of the <u>How To Find God</u> New Testaments, to people

who answered, the others of the group would be praying for us and the contacts being made.

We used a very simple script:

"Hello, this is Pete Battjes from Triumphant Life Center church. I'm calling tonight because our church cares about our neighbors. Do you have any special needs that I can pray for?"

Often there would be a short pause and either the person would say, "No thank you" or "Yes, I'm facing a difficult situation."

If the person said "No thank you", we simply said, "May Jesus bless you and give you His peace. Have a good night.", then hang up.

If the person said "Yes" and shared their need, we would write it on a 3 x 5 card, and then ask if we could pray with them over the phone.

We always asked permission to pray with them and honored their request. Whether we prayed with them then or not, we ended the call saying, "May Jesus bless you and give you His peace." It is so important to use the name of Jesus, so people know Who is really caring for them. If we just say "God bless you", it is too general and people have a lot of different ideas about who God is. It's clear when we mention Jesus that He is the One intervening.

After the call with a specific need, the card was taken to the group of people praying so they could intercede further.

With each card we had the name, address and phone number from the phone directory. In two weeks, we would call those people back to see if they would like continued prayer.

If we got an answering machine when we called the first time, we would simply leave the same message and the church phone number. This way if they desired to contact us for prayer, they could, and some did. We never knew who we were going to talk to or the response we would get.

People were polite and appreciative because we were not overbearing. We just simply offered to serve them. If their hearts were open and ready, we simply took the opportunity. This was the Spirit's work and we discovered which ones were receptive to Him.

There were some crucial contacts made, where people were in real crisis. They were dealing with situations that were causing trauma in their life. We offered hope and comfort through the love and power of Jesus.

In all the calls we made, we never invited someone to come to our church. I didn't believe we were supposed to. Although, in talking to people, some said, "I've never heard of a church doing this before, may I come to your church?"

Again, the Holy Spirit was working, and we simply gave them the information so they might come. This was a faith-growing experience for all of us involved. Our church, those calling, and those in the prayer group who continued covering us, were blessed in this ministry.

THE INVITATION

God is continually bringing forth new spiritual "tools" from a variety of sources to proclaim the gospel to our world. One such tool was a CD entitled – "The Invitation". It was produced in 2006 by Pastor Rick Warren, author of The Purpose Driven Life, along with Maranatha Music and LifeWay Christian Stores. It was an incredible means of presenting Christ. Rick asks the simple question – "What on earth am I here for?' and then he shares spiritual insights. There were contemporary songs mixed in with the various "talks" by Rick.

One million of these CD's were produced for distribution to non-believers. I discovered that they were available for $1.00 each at LifeWay Bookstores in our area.

The church I was serving at the time purchased hundreds of them for the people to "sow" into the lives of family, friends, neighbors, classmates, and work associates. What an inexpensive tool to communicate the truth of God. People gladly received them because they didn't have to read anything, they could put it in their CD player and enjoy listening at home or in the car. I believe this tool was powerfully used by the Holy Spirit to draw people to Christ, but it took people willing to invest and pass them out.

On the CD, Rick had a section called – "Accept, Believe and Receive", then also an "Invitation Prayer". Praise God for this special means of fulfilling the great assignment. Heaven has recorded the full impact of this outreach tool!

GIVING OUT HOPE!

For the past several years the Billy Graham Evangelistic Association has produced excellent short videos to show in churches and give away.

These have been very impacting with topics such as "The Cross", "Heaven" and "Value of A Soul". The church I am serving currently first had a public viewing of the presentation and invited the community to come. Then, we gave DVD's to our members to give away. These can be ordered for $1.00 from www.myhope.org.

Again, ask the Holy Spirit how many you should get and who you should give the DVD to as a gift. It may be a neighbor, relative, work associate, postal service person, grocery clerk, UPS person, gas station attendant or whoever.

I have been amazed at how receptive people are to something they can listen to or watch on their own time. The testimonies and message speak to a person's heart and offer hope through Jesus Christ.

Simple, yes! Life-changing, yes!

POPSICLE SURPRISE

Don't you just love to surprise people, in a good way? The Holy Spirit loves to get us to look and think "outside the box".

A church in the Snoqualmie Valley where I had served previously, felt the Holy Spirit calling them to give away popsicles to kids and parents at a city soccer field close to the church.

One Sunday they filled coolers with popsicles and took them to a soccer field to give away. The people of that church saw the opportunity and were willing to "Go…". Along with the treats, they handed out a simple card with a bright yellow smiley face on it, that said:

<u>We hope we have brightened your day</u>!

*We want you to know that God loves you
and cares about you.*

*If we can ever be of assistance,
please contact us:*

***Raging River Community Church
Preston, Washington***

(425 - _ _ _ - _ _ _ _)

The Holy Spirit can use something as practical as giving away popsicles on a Sunday afternoon with a simple information card, to touch someone's heart and draw them to Jesus and His Church.

Sometimes the simpler, the better. It's a little investment that gets a lot of attention and has a special impact.

TRUTH AT THE TRAILHEAD

I used to live on a road where there was a hiking trailhead and parking area close to my house. I had driven by this area many times coming and going. One day, the Spirit prompted me to leave gospel tracts on the windshields of the cars parked there. He wanted me to plant seeds of truth that would be found and read by those enjoying the beauty of God's creation.

As I was contemplating this new assignment, a pastor friend of mine just happen to share some information at a weekly Pastor's Prayer group that I attended. He said that there is a ministry called The Pocket Testament League that will send a person 30 Gospel of John booklets a month to give away. Their mission is to have believers give away the Gospel and use this means to fulfill the Great Commission.

So far, they have had millions of these Gospel booklets distributed through people around the world. I went to the website and found that various covers are available. I noticed one that had the title, "God's Great Outdoors" with a picture of a beautiful mountain scene on the cover.

This was my new tool for bring God's truth to people who park at the trailhead. I even asked a friend to get a supply of 30 booklets for me with the same cover, so I could put at least 60 of these on the parked cars each month. What could the Holy Spirit do with this? He loves to reveal Jesus to our world and this was a prime opportunity.

The first page of the booklet has the following information in bold letters –

YOU'RE HOLDING IN YOUR HANDS A TRUE STORY. An eyewitness account that has stood the test of time and made a difference to millions of lives around the world. It is a story that will help you sort through the priorities of your life and answer your deepest questions, ones we all struggle with. Like "Where did I come from?" and "Why am I here?" and "Where am I going?"

On the back there is contact information for those who want to know more. The amazing thing is, this kingdom ministry was originally inspired by the vision of a teenage girl. Isn't that awesome?

The Holy Spirit can use children, teenagers, and adults to fulfill the great assignment of Jesus. Check out the website at: www.ptl.org.

What's important is for you personally to be asking the Holy Spirit to show you ways that you can be His instrument to fulfill the great assignment and see lost people come to Jesus either directly through your witness or indirectly through other means.

We are involved in an incredible adventure with Jesus in sharing His Gospel. We each have a very significant part and are included in His plan. Never underestimate what the Spirit can use to reach people who may have resisted Him for years, but may be open due to a crisis in their life. Often, when people come to the end of themselves, they are willing to consider Jesus.

FREE PRAYER

A fellow-pastor, who serves in a Vineyard Church in the University District of Seattle, shared with me how the Holy Spirit led them in a prayer outreach. A number of those in the congregation set up a simple stand on a busy street corner with a large sign – "**FREE PRAYER**". It was encouraging to see how many people actually stopped and asked for prayer!

The Spirit loves to work in simple ways to connect believers with those who don't know Jesus but have a great need in their life. Some are lonely people needing to talk to someone else. Others are curious and interested in finding out what this is all about. Then there are those who are searching and want to find answers that will give them purpose in living. If we are open, God's Spirit will reveal how we are to connect with lost people and let our light shine for the One who is the Light of the world.

Jesus is the One who said, *"Let your light shine before men in such a way that they may see your good works and glorify your Father who is in heaven."* (Matthew 5:16).

Let's do it in Spirit-led ways until He returns in Glory.

"ACT OF KINDNESS" BASKETS

Lighthouse Christian Church continually prays for the Holy Spirit to lead us in community outreach. Someone from the congregation suggested that we reach out to our closest neighbors with "Act of Kindness" baskets.

These baskets were filled with special gifts, like a gift card to a local coffee shop and other thoughtful items. Since it was close to Valentine's Day, each basket included special chocolate candies in a heart shaped box. We also felt the Holy Spirit leading us to include a DVD entitled "Heaven". We printed up a special card thanking the people we were bringing the baskets to, for being our neighbors and included a list of some basic ministries of the church.

On a specific day, teams of two people went out and delivered the baskets personally. Our neighbors were so surprised and appreciative of our thoughtfulness. We even received special "Thank You" cards in the mail from some of the recipients.

We never know when we make a connection where it may lead in the future. Sometimes it's just a matter of looking around the community and asking, "How can I reach someone in a very practical way?"

It's important for churches to look at who is in their community and consider how they are to serve people. When we do this, it gets people's attention!

The Holy Spirit is creative – after all He was part of creating the world and making it beautiful. He can use us to do creative, beautiful things for others as well.

BLUEGRASS & BBQ FESTIVAL

People love music and food – they are a great mix, especially outside in the beauty of God's creation.

The Lighthouse Christian Church is located on the Oregon Coast Highway in a rural area between two small towns. A lot of people drive by, but it is not a heavily populated area around the church itself.

When I came to the church, I began asking the Holy Spirit how we can build a bridge into our community. He put on my heart to have a Bluegrass Music Festival with a BBQ for free. The Elders were in agreement that we should set a date and begin planning.

A member of the church knew of a group named, The Bethel Mountain Band in another part of Oregon. I contacted them and they were excited about coming to play and sing for Jesus. A family from our church offered to participate, as well as a gifted musician who had just moved to the area and had started attending the church.

The Lord was lining it all up, including the cooks for the BBQ. We even added a large bouncy castle and games for the children. Church members got on board and donated potato salad, chips, watermelon and drinks.

We advertised on our church sign, printed up large posters and small flyers to distribute, as well as put ads in the local paper.

When the day came, we were amazed at the new faces that showed up. Approximately 200 or more came and we connected with our community in a special way. We were blessed to see a couple vans of physically challenged people drive up and join us. We want our community to know we are "people-friendly".

The next year we added a Kids Carnival, with inflatable slides and game booths. What fun this provided!

The Holy Spirit wants us to demonstrate that Christ-followers enjoy having a good time and can relate to others. It's a great way to build a bridge into a community.

LAUNDRY LOVE

How would you like to surprise and encourage someone by paying for their clothes to be washed and dried?

There are believers in Seaside, OR who do just that. They pick a night, make coffee, get donuts and go to the local laundry mat – they also take lots of quarters for the machines.

They offer refreshments to people who come in and then offer to pay to have two loads of their clothes washed and dried.

People are amazed and grateful.

This gives these believers an opportunity to connect with those who come in and listen to their life-story. It's incredible how much people will share if they encounter others who truly care and will listen.

Simple, sincere, and Spirit-led!

ROSES FOR PROSTITUTES

What a powerful impact one church in a major city had when the Holy Spirit led them to reach out to prostitutes. These believers wanted to do what Jesus did – show the love and compassion of the Father.

They were led to buy beautiful red roses and then go out on a specific night in teams of two or three to the heart of their city.

When they encountered a prostitute, they simply offered her a rose and said, "Jesus loves you and cares about you and so do we".

Often the women given a rose would begin to cry. They would be invited to come to the church and find a place of safety and help.

Caring Christ-followers who were willing to reach out to those enslaved in a life of sin, made the love of God real. They didn't condemn these women, they offered compassion – love in action! The beautiful rose was a special gift as well.

It involves some time and effort, but it is following Jesus' example.

There is a church in Seattle called "Strip Church". Those who have been rescued from this life-style show up and bring cupcakes to strippers and bouncers at the different clubs in the city. They reach out to them in a caring way and invite them to experience God's love. They know from personal experience what it is like to be spiritually empty and hopeless.

Isn't it so true that people don't care how much you know until they know how much you care?

Instant Replay in Heaven?

God shows amazing grace in the ways He reaches out to us. In light of the fact that He rescued us so we might be children of God, we should also have a passion for those who do not know Jesus as Savior. Jesus made it clear that we are to be "salt" and "light" in our world to point others to Him. This is our on-going great assignment.

The Holy Spirit will continue to be involved in convergence experiences in our lives. May we recognize them and make the most of every opportunity to lift Jesus Christ up as Savior and Lord to a dying world.

What excites me is the possibility that when we graduate into Glory and abide in the presence of God for all eternity, He may reveal to us – like an instant replay – the many different ways that we were part of His work to touch people's hearts and lives. What great joy that would bring!

But, just knowing that we are doing this as His ambassadors, because of our love and devotion to Him, makes this a delight now.

As Christ-followers we can cach look back over our past and identify the people or things the Holy Spirit used to draw us to Jesus. We each have a witness to share with our world that testifies of the Father's faithfulness to us through Jesus.

Keep praying for the Spirit to show you "new things" to connect with people who need to know Christ and the way of everlasting life.

The Spirit *Without* Measure

There is so much more in the Scriptures that could be discussed regarding the Holy Spirit. It is there for you to continue discovering in the days ahead.

A statement made by John the Baptizer in John 3:34 is worth reflecting on as I conclude. It is this revelation:

> *"For He whom God has sent speaks the words of God; for He gives the Spirit without measure."*

The NIV Study Bible commentators note – "Some hold that it is only to Jesus that the Spirit is given without limit. Others take the "He" as a reference to Christ's giving the Spirit without limit to believers." [9]

I agree with the latter view, that Jesus as the One Who "gives the Spirit without measure"! He is not limited as to who receives God's Spirit.

Jesus, the Son, the Father, and the Holy Spirit are One God. Therefore He is complete already. We are the ones who need the divine impartation or convergence in our lives.

When we accept Christ by faith, we will have all of the Holy Spirit. The real question remains – "Does He have all of us?". That is an on-going matter of submission, as has been mentioned before.

I believe this revelation about Jesus in John 3:34 ties in directly with the prophecy found in Isaiah 44:3 (NIV) –
"... I will pour out my Spirit on your offspring, and my blessing on your descendants." Which also ties in with Isaiah 32:15 (NIV) that states, *"till the Spirit is poured upon us from on high...".*

Both prophecies point to the coming of the Messiah and the work He will accomplish. This is confirmed by Joel 2:28 (NIV) – *"... I will pour out my Spirit on all people..."* and fulfilled only by Jesus Christ!

Jim Cymbala shares the following insight on the outpouring of the Spirit:

"We can never do what the Spirit can do. No amount of human talent and exertion of energy will ever grow the spiritual kingdom of Christ. We need to return to depending on the Spirit's fire, which not only quickens and penetrates but also illuminates our path." [10]

He also challenges those in the body of Christ regarding a mindset that hinders us:

"Some of us are afraid of opening up to the Holy Spirit because we prefer to stay in control. That's under-standable. We're concerned about self-preservation, so giving up control can be scary. We're not sure we're comfortable with what God did in Acts 2 when people spoke in languages they had never learned. At the time, the early Christians' manifestations of euphoric joy and ecstatic utterances made people mocking say, 'Those people are drunk!' And we see their point. Why would God inspire such a holy bedlam? Many of us want more of God but not to the point of being ridiculed. Our Western minds think, I will serve the Lord, but I will remain in control as I do it. But whether we like it or not, that's not how the church began. The church began with Spirit-controlled Christians who yielded themselves to God. That's radical, yes, but that's the way the Lord did it…The irony of Spirit-filled living is that we have to give up power in order to gain a greater power." [11]

Jesus boldly stated that He was the fulfillment of Isaiah 61:1-2. Luke 4:18-19 confirms this.

Now, through the fullness of *"the Spirit without measure"* given to us by Jesus, we can continue His work to *"preach good news to the poor…proclaim freedom for the prisoners…recovery of sight to the blind…release the oppressed...proclaim the year of the Lord's favor."* (Isaiah 61:1-2).

I challenge you to go to John 14:16-26; 16:5-15 and let Jesus speak to you personally about the work of the Holy Spirit in your life.

Go away for several hours by yourself to a special spot where you won't be distracted. Give the Lord the opportunity to move you forward in grasping the significance of His will for you.

Read these Scriptures several times and take notes of all Jesus is saying and how it applies to you.

Let His revelation of the Holy Spirit bring a zeal and passion to pursue Him every day.

As believers in Jesus, we have the Holy Spirit in us. We have so much to live for as we continue to know Him and make Him known through the leading and power of the Holy Spirit.

As a means of on-going encouragement each month, I would recommend subscribing to *Charisma* – LIFE IN THE SPIRIT, a magazine that continue to reveal how God's Spirit is moving currently (charismamag.com).

We can expect Him to fulfill the plan and purposes of the Lord...and involve us!

I believe it is most fitting to conclude this book with the special invitation of the Holy Spirit and Jesus in the final words of Scripture:

"I, <u>Jesus</u>, have sent My angel to testify to you these things for the churches. I am the root and the descendant of David, the bright morning star.

<u>The Spirit and the bride</u> say, 'Come.' And let the one who hears say, 'Come.' And let the one who is thirsty come; let the one who wishes take the water of life without cost…

He who testifies to these things says, 'Yes, I am coming quickly.' Amen. Come, Lord Jesus." (Revelation 22:16-17, 20)

May this be your sincere prayer until Jesus returns in all His glory with His angels to receive you unto Himself forever – ***"Come, Lord Jesus".***

"Do not put out the Spirit's fire;"

Apostle Paul
(I Thessalonians 5:19 NIV)

Appendix A

"Thank you, Father, for Vivian and Peter. Lord, for the wonderful anointing on their lives and this anointing also means the breaking of every yoke put on them by mankind.

You've been at times under man's yokes and the Lord has caused you to walk away from that and say, 'Lord, we belong to you' and you have made a new and fresh clean start, it seems like. And the Lord has said, 'This is a clean start and you are turning a corner, a significant one as well, and that significant corner is going to lead you into your inheritance. It's going to lead you into the 'more of God' that you've always desired, that somehow you've been kept from having. And the Lord says, 'I'm going to cause you to take this inheritance, I'm going to cause you to, to step into that inheritance, to step into the very fulfilling of the plans I've called you to. This is the beginning of it, this is the beginning of it and the Lord says, 'Don't you ever fear'!

You will not go back to where you've come from. You're not going to go back to where you've come from, this is definitely a turn for the better. I mean, not that it was bad where you've come from, but its' never been that place what you knew God had in the Spirit and this is about for you to take place, friend.

Peter, God has put a dream in your heart. God has put something in your heart and the Lord says, 'You go after that' and it's not going to be an easy thing, but who said it's going to be easy. But, you know it's your calling and it's your destiny and you're going to go with it and you will rejoice in doing so.

Full faith and full confidence that God enables you to do what He is calling you to do and what you thought you had lost over the past years in terms even of anointing, in terms of what God has given you initially. You've wondered about that...'will I ever have that back' and the Lord says to you, 'you'll not just have that back, but you'll have much better back', like He's going to return it to you but with a much greater intensity and with a much greater ability and with a much greater blessing than you've ever thought would be possible. Set your sights high because what the Lord has in mind is far beyond your natural capability.

And Vivian, you're very much a part of that, it's not just Peter, but it's both of you. It's both of you working under the yoke that He places over you and on you, it's a yoke that's easy, not heavy. It's a yoke that's easy to carry, the burden is easy, it's not difficult, it's the yoke that fits you, it's the yoke that He came to give, it's like this yoke He puts on you and the anointing enables you to have and together, both of you have a very powerful ministry in God.

I don't know what you're doing or what you've done, but I sense the Lord is going to do something far beyond your natural grasp.   You're in for a good time, thank the Holy Spirit!

Appendix B

A Brief Statement on the Holy Spirit
North Sound Church - Edmonds, Washington

The following is a statement produced to bring clarity and understanding so that everyone can know where this fellowship stands regarding Scripture and the Holy Spirit. It may be helpful for you personally and also worth adopting in your church.

At North Sound Church we believe that there is one living and true God, eternally existing in three persons; Father, Son, and Holy Spirit (Matthew 28:19; John 1:1-4; I John 5:7). We believe the Holy Spirit came forth from the Father and the Son to convict the world of sin, righteousness, and judgment, and to regenerate, sanctify, and empower all who believe in Christ and that He is an abiding Helper, Teacher and Guide (John 16:7-15; Romans 8:14-17; Ephesians 1:13, 14; John 14:26).

We believe that the baptism in the Holy Spirit is a part of the process of conversion and that all who are followers of Jesus Christ have received the Holy Spirit (I Corinthians 12:13; Romans 8:9; see also Mark 1:8; Luke 3:16; John 1:33; Acts 2:38; 11:16-17).

The Scriptures speak of the early believers being filled with the Holy Spirit. This was not a one-time experience, as the same believers could be filled with the Spirit on more than one occasion (Acts 2:4; 4:8; 4:31; 9:17; 13:52). Paul speaks of the need for believers to continually allow the Holy Spirit to fill them (Ephesians 5:18). God's desire is that all believers live in the fullness of the Spirit.

We believe that all of the gifts of the Holy Spirit are available for the common good of the body of Christ, the church (I Corinthians 12:7). They should be administered in an environment of mutual respect for the place of the various gifts in the body (Romans 12:3-8; I Corinthians 12:1-31). It is important to encourage each person in the congregation to discover the gifts of the Spirit that have been received and to use them to build up the church.

The early church worshipped in both the temple courts and in homes (Acts 2:46-47). Worship in homes seems to have been an informal gathering in which each one could share a hymn, a word of teaching, a revelation, a tongue or an interpretation (I Corinthians 14:26). The expression of verbal gifts did not assume that every word was from God, but rather that the words that were given needed to be discerned (I Corinthians 14:29). The Scriptures are clear that one has control over one's use of the gifts (I Corinthians 14:32). At North Sound Church we believe that the place for the expression of the verbal gifts of the Spirit is the prayer meeting, as the discernment that is necessary is difficult to provide in the context of a church service.

There are seasons in the history of the church where the Holy Spirit has been poured out in unusually powerful ways. At such times normal protocols for services seem to be set aside in a desire to flow with what the Spirit is doing in the congregation. At North Sound Church we want to be open to the work of the Holy Spirit in these special times, but believe that these times are not generated by human manipulation, but rather by God's sovereignty. We believe that these seasons will be self-evident.

In both the major passages of Scripture dealing with the gifts of the Spirit, the importance of love is articulated (Romans 12:9a; I Corinthians 13:1-13). The building up of the church, characterized by love for one another, should be reflected in the manifestation of the gifts of the Spirit in the church.

Appendix C

<u>Holy Spirit Devotionals that Inspire</u>

The following devotions are taken from Anne Graham Lotz book, <u>The Joy Of My Heart</u>, which is a compilation of meditations taken from her other books and put into a daily devotional. These specific ones highlight the Holy Spirit and His impact on us. They've greatly inspired me. May they touch your heart as well.

FEBRUARY 19
FILLED WITH THE SPIRIT

"Be filled with the Spirit."
EPHESIANS 5:18 NIV

God has clearly commanded you and me to "be filled with the Spirit." But an un-confessed sin or resistance to His authority will block the "flow" of His life within us. If we do not deal with it, our spiritual lives become stagnant and we lose our attractiveness and usefulness to God. And we have nothing refreshing about us that would draw other people to Christ.

What is hindering you from being filled with the Holy Spirit? To be filled with the Holy Spirit is to be under His moment-by-moment control. He has not been given to you so that you can keep Him confined to a particular area in your life. Let Him loose! He is Lord! The amount of power you experience to live a victorious, triumphant Christian life is directly proportional to the freedom you give the Spirit to be Lord of your life!

(p. 62)   *Just Give Me Jesus*

JULY 31
ANOTHER COUNSELOR

"I will ask the Father; and he will give you another Counselor to be with you forever – the Spirit of truth."
JOHN 14:16-17 NIV

Jesus described the Holy Spirit as "Another." The Greek word actually means "another who is exactly the same." So although the Holy Spirit is a distinct person, He is exactly the same as Jesus, but without the physical body.

We know that Jesus is in heaven. As the first martyr, Stephen, was being stoned to death, he looked up and saw heaven open and Jesus standing at God's right hand, preparing to welcome him home! (Acts 7:56) But that doesn't mean Jesus has left us to stumble through the darkness of the future on our own. He promised His disciples that when He went to heaven, He would ask His Father to send down to earth "Another." Jesus called Him the Counselor (John 14:16), because He is readily available to give us wisdom for our decisions, direction for our future, and management for our responsibilities.

(p. 232)   *Just Give Me Jesus*

AUGUST 18
EQUIPPED TO SERVE

*"There are different kinds of gifts, but the same Spirit.
There are different kinds of service, but the same
Lord."*
I CORINTHIANS 12:4-5 NIV

What God commands you and me to do, He equips us for. It's that simple!

If you want to discover your spiritual gifts, start obeying God. Responding to His command with "I can't" is invalid, because He will never command you to do something that He has not equipped and empowered you to do. As you serve Him, you will find that He has given you the gifts that are necessary to follow through in obedience. Any of them. All of them. And if you lack any that you need, God will bring people alongside you to have the gifts that you don't. Working together, you will accomplish the task to the glory of God.

And that's the body of Christ! That's the church. Individual members of the family, each obeying his or her call, exercising the particular gifts the Spirit has given, so that our work is not in vain but produces eternal results. So...get to work! You're equipped!

(p. 251)   *Just Give Me Jesus*

AUGUST 30
THE SPIRIT OF TRUTH

"When he, the Spirit of truth, comes,
he will guide you into all truth."
JOHN 16:13 NIV

The Holy Spirit is so identified with the Bible, one of His names is Truth! In fact, Peter reveals that the Holy Spirit is the inspirational Author of the Old Testament Scriptures. (2 Pet. 1:20-21) And Paul wrote to Timothy, encouraging him to stay in the Scriptures because, "all Scripture is God-breathed," referring once again to the Spirit-inspired Word of God (2 Tim. 3:16, NIV).

Have you been trying to work up some kind of emotional feeling? If you lack "it," have you *felt* you didn't have the Holy Spirit? The Holy Spirit is the Spirit of Truth, which means He always works according to and through the Word of God whether you *feel* Him or not. Have you been seeking some ecstatic experience, thinking that would be the Holy Spirit? Remember that He never acts independently; He always works through *the* Truth – the living Word of God, Who is Jesus, and the written Word of God, which is your Bible.

(p. 263)   *Just Give Me Jesus*

338

SEPTEMBER 6
GOD'S GUARENTEE

"I will pray the Father, and He will give you another Helper, that He may abide with you forever."
JOHN 14:16 NKJV

The same Spirit that hovered over the surface of the deep in the second verse of the Bible is the same Spirit that fully indwelt Jesus Christ. (John 3:34) In John 14 Jesus speaks of Him as the Spirit of truth, (John 14:17) because He always works through the truth, which is incarnate in Christ and written in the Scriptures. (2 Pet. 1:21-22) He is also referred to as the Counselor because He gives wisdom, direction for living, and understanding of truth. (John 14:16) And He is called the Holy Spirit because He is totally separate from sin. (John 14:26)

This wonderful Spirit of God is available to live within you when you repent of your sin and, by faith, invite Jesus Christ to come into your life as your Lord and Savior. (John 14:17) In fact, without the "seal" of His Presence in your life, you have no eternal credibility with the Father. (Eph. 1:13) But with the "seal" of His Presence you have the guarantee of a heavenly home and all the blessings of God.

(p. 271) *God's Story*

OCTOBER 16
OUR FATHER COMES ALONGSIDE

"If we live in the Spirit, let us also walk in the Spirit"
GALATIANS 5:25 NKJV

The Greek word for "comforter" is *parakletos,* which literally means one called alongside to help. This was beautifully illustrated in the 1996 Summer Olympics. As the runners in the 440-meter race flew around the track, one of them suddenly pulled up on the back stretch, and limped to a stop. He had pulled a hamstring! As the crowd stood, holding its collective breath, a man ran out of the stands to the young athlete. It was his father! As the television crew relayed the moving scene to the watching world, the microphones picked up the runner's words: "Dad, you've got to help me across the finish line. I've trained all my life for this race." And so the father put his arm around his son, and together, they limped across the finish line to a standing ovation!

In the race of life, our heavenly Father has come alongside us through the Holy Spirit. And when we think we can't go one more step He puts His everlasting arms around us, and gently walks with us to the finish.

(p. 313)   *Just Give Me Jesus*

Appendix D

Bill Bright – Founder of Campus Crusade for Christ. Some of his closing words at the end of his book: "Blessed Child"

"It is the truth that God is indeed alive and still moves in supernatural ways today, whenever He so desires and for His purposes, through the lives of those who love, trust, and obey Him. It's the truth that the source of God's power is found in His Son, Jesus Christ, and in the Holy Spirit, not in man's devices. It's the truth that what we see with our own eyes on a day-to-day basis isn't the half of it. There is indeed a supernatural reality all around us that is just as real as the world we see.

And most importantly, it's the truth that, when seen through spiritual eyes, a healed heart and transformed life are far more spectacular than a straightened hand or restored sight. These were the themes of the New Testament church, and they must be the themes that guide our lives today. As dedicated believers, we are on a grand adventure that bristles with power and excitement. But I have been saddened again and again at the lack of enthusiasm and zeal among many who claim to be His followers. A lack of first love among His body – the Church.

The Bible explains that in the last days people will hold to a form of godliness while denying its power (2 Timothy 3:5). Sadly, many believers do not know the reality of living a supernatural life through the enabling power of the Holy Spirit...The power of the Holy Spirit characterized the New Testament church no less than it did the lives of the prophets of old. The Lord enabled them to do many miraculous signs and wonders (Acts 14:3), many were healed (Acts 5:16), others were raised from the dead (Acts 9:41), and most importantly the good news of Christ began to spread throughout the world.

Jesus said, except you become as a little child, you cannot enter the kingdom of God. Children are generally trusting and dependable and believe what they are told. At Campus Crusade for Christ we have noticed that the response in many parts of the world to the *Jesus Film* is phenomenal. Audiences who see the film say that if Jesus can heal the blind, He can heal them too. And so He does. In fact, we have reported situations where people have actually been raised from the dead, and their communities revolutionized by the message that resulted.

But in the Western world we are more prone to rationalize and analyze until the true meaning of the gospel is dissipated and often rendered powerless. We become like the churches of Ephesus and Laodicea: we have left our first love and are neither hot nor cold. We find it difficult to believe that Jesus would do today what He did centuries ago, while many of our fellow believers across the seas do believe, and they rejoice in the fruits of their belief.

Without the Holy Spirit, our own strivings are fruitless. It is "Not by might nor by power, but by my Spirit," says the Lord (Zechariah 4:6). The last instruction Jesus gave to His disciples on the Mount of Olives was to wait in Jerusalem until they were renewed with power from on high. "You will receive power when the Holy Spirit comes on you; and you will be my witnesses in Jerusalem, and in all Judea and Samaria, and to the ends of the earth" (Acts 1:8).

Everything in the Christian life involves the Holy Spirit. The Holy Spirit came to glorify Christ, to lead us into all truth, to convict us of sin, and to draw us to the Savior (John 16). We must be born of the Spirit (John 3). Only through the enabling of the Spirit can a person understand the Word of God and live under its power…No book written by man can begin to capture every aspect of the remarkable truths about the Holy Spirit…"

Bill Bright

Notes

Chapter One
Understanding Convergence

1. James Strong, *Strong's Exhaustive Concordance of the Bible – A Concise Dictionary of the Words in The Hebrew Bible with their Renderings in the Authorized English Version* (McLeaan, VA: Mac Donald Publishing Company), p. 107 (#7307 – wind, breath, mind, spirit).

2. Ibid., p. 58 (#4151 – breath, ghost, life, spirit, mind).

Chapter Two
Knowing the Holy Spirit

1. W.E. Vine, *Vine's Expository Dictionary of the Old and New Testament Words* (Iowa Falls, IA: World Bible Publishers, 1981), p. 208.

Chapter Three
The Impact of the Holy Spirit in the Old Testament

1. Henry Blackaby, Richard Blackaby, *Experiencing God Day by Day* (Nashville, TN: B & H Publishing, 2006), 247.

Chapter Four
The Impact of the Holy Spirit in the New Testament

1. Jim Cymbala, *SPIRIT RISING: Tapping Into The Power of the Holy Spirit* (Grand Rapids, MI: Zondervan, 2012), p. 72.

Chapter Five
Attributes of the Holy Spirit

1. Greg Laurie, *How To Find God New Testament* (Carol Streams, IL: Tyndale House Publishers, Inc., 1996), p. 120.
2. Francis Chan, *Remembering the Forgotten God – An Interactive Workbook for Individual or Small Group Study* (Colorado Springs, CO: David C. Cook, 2010) p. 92.
3. Henry Blackaby, Richard Blackaby, *Experiencing God Day by Day*, p. 344.
4. Greg Laurie, *How To Find God New Testament*, p. 228.

Chapter Six
The Fruit of the Spirit

1. Jack W. Hayford, Spirit Filled Life Bible (Nashville, TN: Thomas Nelson Publishers, 1991), p. 1780.
2. Ronald A. Beers, *Life Application Bible* (Wheaton, IL: Tyndale House Publishers, Inc., 1987), p. 487.
3. Ibid.
4. Kenneth Barker, The NIV Study Bible (Grand Rapids, MI: Zondervan Bible Publishers, 1985), p. 1787.

5. Anne Graham Lotz, The Joy of My Heart (Nashville, TN: Thomas Nelson, Inc., 2004), p. 226.

6. Ronald A. Beers, *Life Application Bible*, p. 487.

7. Kenneth Barker, *The NIV Study Bible,* p. 1475.

8. Used by permission: Mark Rogers, Kenmore Community Church, Kenmore, WA.

9. Spiros Zodhiates, *The Complete Word Study New Testament* (Chattanooga, TN: AMG Publishers, 1991), p. 952.

10. Ibid., p. 866.

11. Henry Blackaby, Richard Blackaby, *Experiencing God Day by Day*, p. 334.

12. Anne Graham Lotz, *The Joy Of My Heart,* p. 209.

13. Ronald A. Beers, *Life Application Bible*, p. 487.

Chapter Seven
The Ministry Gifts of the Spirit

1. John C. Maxwell, *The Maxwell Leadership Bible* (Nashville, TN: Thomas Nelson Publishers, 2002), p. 1533.

2. Ibid.

3. Hayford, *The Spirit Filled Life Bible*, p. 2025.

4. Ibid., p. 2025-26.

Chapter Eight
The Motivational Gifts of the Spirit

1. John C. Maxwell, *The Maxwell Leadership Bible*, p. 1381.

2. Ibid.

3. Jack W. Hayford, *The Spirit Filled Life Bible*, p. 2023.

4. Ibid., p. 2023-24.

Chapter Nine
The Manifestation Gifts of the Spirit

1. Larry Sparks and Troy Anderson, *The Healing Miracles Preacher*, Charisma Media (Lake Mary, FL, 2015) p. 22.

2. Jack W. Hayford, *The Spirit Filled Bible*, p. 1739.

3. Ibid., p. 2024.

4. Fran Lance, *You Can Minister in the Spiritual Gifts* (Seattle, WA: Free Lance Ministries, 1994). p. 68

5. Jack W. Hayford, *The Spirit Filled Bible*, p. 2024.

6. Ibid., p. 2025.

7. Ibid., p. 2024.

8. Kenneth Barker, *The NIV Study Bible*, p. 1750.

9. Jack W. Hayford, *The Spirit Filled Bible*, p. 2024.

10. Ibid., p. 2025.

11. Ibid.

12. Kenneth Barker, *The NIV Study Bible*, p. 1669.

13. Ibid., p. 1926.

14. John C. Maxwell, *The Maxwell Leadership Bible*, p. 1403.

15. Francis Chan, *Remembering the Forgotten God – An Interactive Workbook for Individual or Small Group Study,* p. 21.

Chapter Ten
The Unique Filling of the Spirit

1. Jack W. Hayford, *The Spirit Filled Life Bible*, p. 1613.
2. Ibid. p. 1588.
3. Kenneth Barker, *The NIV Study Bible*, p. 1798.
4. Jack W. Hayford, *The Spirit Filled Bible*, p. 1794.
5. Fran Lance, *You Can Minister in the Spiritual Gifts*, p. 27.
6. Kenneth Barker, *The NIV Study Bible*, p. 1645.
7. Jack W. Hayford, *The Spirit Filled Bible*, p. 1640.
8. Kenneth Barker, *The NIV Study Bible*, p. 1683.
9. Ibid., p. 1795.
10. Ibid., p. 1750-51.
11. Ibid.
12. Ibid. p. 1844

Chapter Eleven
Fulfilling the Great Assignment

1. Francis Chan, *Remembering the Forgotten God – An Interactive Workbook for Individual or Small Group Study*, p. 91.
2. Chuck Quinley, *I Want To Bear Fruit* (Doraville, GA: Chuck Quinley, 2000), p. 79.
3. Francis Chan, *Remembering the Forgotten God – An Interactive Workbook for Individual or Small Group Study*, p. 11.
4. Ibid., p. 12.
5. Jim Cymbala, *SPIRIT RISING: Tapping Into The Power of the Holy Spirit*, p. 37-38.
6. Ibid., p. 38.

7. Ibid., p. 39-40.
8. Francis Chan, *Remembering the Forgotten God – An Interactive Workbook for Individual or Small Group Study,* p. 105.
9. Kenneth Barker, *The NIV Study Bible*, p. 1599.
10. Jim Cymbala, *SPIRIT RISING: Tapping Into The Power of the Holy Spirit,* p. 71.
11. Ibid., p. 40-41

About the Author

PETE BATTJES was born and raised in southern California on a chicken ranch. Upon graduation from High School he moved to Michigan to attend college. He met his wife, Vivian, and married in 1975.

Together they served a rural church in Michigan and were blessed with three children. After serving ten years in pastoral ministry, Pete was led to continue his education at Regent University (Virginia Beach, Virginia). After completing a Master of Biblical Studies, he was led by the Holy Spirit to Seattle, Washington to serve as Northwest Area Director of CBN Ministries.

Pete has since served four other churches of different denominations, as well as, being Director of Church Relations with the Seattle Union Gospel Mission, Director of the Seattle March for Jesus, and Director of the Seattle Urban Pipeline.

He shares in the conviction of the Apostle Paul – *"To the weak I became weak. I have become all things to all men so that by all possible means I might save some. I do all this for the sake of the gospel, that I may share in its blessings."* (I Corinthians 9:22-23 NIV).

Both Pete and Vivian have served with Youth With A Mission in Thailand and the Philippians. Pete serves on the Board of Directors of Discovery Bay YWAM (Port Townsend, Washington) and is a regular DTS guest speaker.

He received his Doctor of Ministry degree from Newburgh Theological Seminary (Newburgh, Indiana) in 2012.

He is a contributing author with the "Kingdom, Power, Glory" project of The Legacy Institute (Kenmore, Washington) and serves on the Board of Directors.

As an ordained minister and servant of the Lord Jesus Christ, his passion is to reach, teach, and release others in Kingdom ministry to fulfill the Great Commission of Jesus through the power of the Holy Spirit.

He enjoys snorkeling, whitewater rafting, and fishing.

Pete and Vivian live on the Oregon coast and have three married children and seven grandchildren, who are a great delight to them.

Contact Information: drpetebattjes@gmail.com